NECESSARY CHRISTIANITY

WHAT JESUS SHOWS
WE MUST BE AND DO

CLAUDE R. ALEXANDER JR.

An imprint of InterVarsity Press
Downers Grove, Illinois

InterVarsity Press
P.O. Box 1400 | Downers Grove, IL 60515-1426
ivpress.com | email@ivpress.com

InterVarsity Press® is the publishing division of InterVarsity Christian Fellowship/USA®. For more information, visit intervarsity.org.

All Scripture quotations, unless otherwise indicated, are taken from the New King James Version®. Copyright © 1982 by Thomas Nelson. Used by permission. All rights reserved.

While any stories in this book are true, some names and identifying information may have been changed to protect the privacy of individuals.

The publisher cannot verify the accuracy or functionality of website URLs used in this book beyond the date of publication.

Cover design and image composite: David Fassett
Interior design: Daniel van Loon

ISBN 978-1-5140-0570-5 (print) | ISBN 978-1-5140-0571-2 (digital)

Printed in the United States of America ♾

Library of Congress Cataloging-in-Publication Data
A catalog record for this book is available from the Library of Congress.

29 28 27 26 25 24 23 22 | 8 7 6 5 4 3 2 1

CONTENTS

Introduction

A LIFE OF THE NECESSARY

There's something about birthdays that end in five or zero that causes us to be more definitive about life. At one of my own recent significant milestones, my life came into the sharpest focus I'd ever experienced. It became clear that I possibly had more years behind me than ahead of me. With that came the liberating realization that I was as grown as anybody else. The only difference between me and someone older was that he or she may have fewer years left than I did. I knew what I would tolerate and what I wouldn't, what I could stand and what I couldn't, and I didn't have to feel bad about it. It became clear to me for whom I existed and for what I existed and the direction toward which I was called. Whoever and whatever couldn't deal with that was not my problem. I was comfortable with who God had called me to be and what God had called me to do.

Maturity shouldn't be equated with age, because age is not a sign of maturity. However, maturity in life brings clarity, certainty, and definition. This is also the case with Christian maturity. Maturity in Christ should result in greater clarity, certainty, and definition. Maturity is about growth, and growth in Christ should produce a clearer understanding of Christ, his claims on our life, and the direction in which he is leading us. It should create a greater certainty about who he is, who we are in him, what we can depend on and expect from him, and the reality of what he has promised and revealed. We should possess a greater definitiveness concerning the life we have with him: its nature, its requirements, its aims and benefits. The more mature we are in Christ, the clearer we should be about him and all aspects of our life with him.

One of the things that becomes increasingly clear to me is that the life to which the Christian is called is a life of necessity. God calls the Christian to live with a sense of the necessary, the obliged, and the required. The person who lives under the lordship of Jesus Christ is the one who seeks to live within the will of God and under the voice of God. We show maturity in this life when we view the lines God draws and the directions God gives as essential, imperative, indispensable, and requisite.

However, this view of life is a challenge to the immature Christian. The immature Christian views life in God and with God the way the world views life—from the standpoint of options. In other words, God's claim on our life is one of the many options we can choose. To the secular humanist and the immature Christian, much of life is random, accidental, and haphazard. The will and way of God are seen as peripheral, not essential. The world says we can negotiate with God. We can strike a compromise with God. We can delay and even deny the call and claims of God on us and for us. The dictates of God are a matter of what we might do and not what we must do. They are possibilities, not necessities.

The immature Christian, like the world, operates from "mightness" as it relates to God, God's will, and God's way. On the contrary, the mature Christian comes to understand that life in God and with God is less about what we could do and more about what we must do. Freedom in Christ does not make God's desire of us and for us optional. Freedom in Christ disentangles us so we are able to respond to that which is necessary for us from God and in God.

God is calling for Christians to grow up in him and realize that he calls us to a life of the necessary. He calls us to realize the "mustness" of our life with him.

As we read about the life of Jesus, we get a sense of "mustness." Throughout the Gospels we hear Jesus say, "I must." We read of Jesus, "He must." We hear Jesus tell his disciples or his audience, "You must." Kingdom living— living under the rule and reign of God—is living with a sense of "must," not "might," in relation to God. Often we focus on the "I am" statements of Jesus; seldom do we focus on the "I must" statements. I believe that if we focus on the "I must" statements, we will come to understand necessary Christianity.

1

I MUST FOCUS

THE NECESSITY OF FOCUS

The Child grew and became strong in spirit, filled with wisdom; and the grace of God was upon Him.

His parents went to Jerusalem every year at the Feast of the Passover. And when He was twelve years old, they went up to Jerusalem according to the custom of the feast. When they had finished the days, as they returned, the Boy Jesus lingered behind in Jerusalem. And Joseph and His mother did not know it; but supposing Him to have been in the company, they went a day's journey, and sought Him among their relatives and acquaintances. So when they did not find Him, they returned to Jerusalem, seeking Him. Now so it was that after three days they found Him in the temple, sitting in the midst of the teachers, both listening to them and asking them questions. And all who heard Him were astonished at His understanding and answers. So when they saw Him, they were amazed; and His mother said to Him, "Son, why have You done this to us? Look, Your father and I have sought You anxiously."

> And He said to them, "Why did you seek Me? Did you not know that I must be about My Father's business?" But they did not understand the statement which He spoke to them.
>
> Then He went down with them and came to Nazareth, and was subject to them, but His mother kept all these things in her heart. And Jesus increased in wisdom and stature, and in favor with God and men. (Luke 2:40-52)

The text before us is familiar. It is the one story we have of Jesus' childhood. The account is bracketed by a description of Jesus. Luke 2:40 reads, "The Child grew and became strong in spirit, filled with wisdom; and the grace of God was upon Him." Luke 2:52 says, "Jesus increased in wisdom and stature, and in favor with God and men." Here Luke speaks about the ever-evolving human character of Jesus. He describes the aspects of maturity in a human sense in terms of life with God in the world.

It is a progressive life. Jesus *grew* and *increased*. These two words provide a layered understanding of Christian growth and maturity. While the word for *grew* speaks specifically to physical growth, the word for *increased* is more layered. It means to beat forward and to lengthen out by hammering, as a metalsmith forges metal. It refers to growth as a result of being stretched and shaped by applied pressure, with some pain being experienced. The word *grew* speaks to enlargement, while the word *increased* speaks to a process of expansion.

There are many who pray for increase (anointing, God-opportunities, prosperity) but who don't understand that they are asking to be stretched and lengthened in a way that requires pressure and may involve pain. To illustrate, there was a period in my teenage years when I experienced extraordinary physiological growth, gaining five inches of height in a matter of weeks. Those weeks and the period immediately following were some of the most painful weeks of my life. It hurt to walk. It hurt to sit. It even hurt to have anything placed on my knees. I was diagnosed with Osgood-Schlatter disease, an inflammation of the bone at the growth plate about two inches below the kneecap, where the tendon attaches the thigh to the leg. The thigh muscles pull the tendon on the bone whenever the leg is bent or straightened. The tendon rubs against the bone and creates the inflammation. The growth spurt included and produced growth pain. The process of increase included the friction inherent in stretching. Praying for increase includes praying to be stretched and to experience friction. If we can't take the stretching, friction, and inflammation, we shouldn't pray for increase.

Jesus grew and increased. He was made strong in spirit. His life in the Spirit strengthened him. He acquired wisdom. God's grace, delight, and pleasure governed his life. He increased in wisdom, stature, and favor with God and with men. Christian maturity entails continued strengthening in the Spirit and by the Spirit, growth in wisdom and in grace.

Within the bracket statements concerning Jesus' maturity, we have the story of Jesus in the temple. Luke tells us that Joseph, Mary, and Jesus had gone to Jerusalem to attend the feast of the Passover. Jesus was twelve years of age. He was one year from his bar mitzvah, when he would be recognized as a son of the covenant. He would be recognized as fully responsible to God and for his life with God. At the end of the Passover, Joseph and Mary head home, each of them assuming Jesus is with the other. However, Jesus has lingered in Jerusalem. After a day of journeying, Joseph and Mary discover that Jesus is missing. They search for him. After three days they find Jesus in the temple in Jerusalem talking with the teachers of the law. Mary asks him, "Why have you done this to us? Look, Your father and I have sought You anxiously." Jesus responds, "Why did you seek Me? Did you not know that I must be about My Father's business?"

When Mary informs Jesus that she and Joseph have anxiously and frantically searched for him, Jesus responds by asking them why they have searched for him. His absence from them should not have resulted in his being lost to them. They should have known where to look. He raises the question of their having to search for him based on their not knowing what he must be about. "Did you not know that I must be about My Father's business?" They lost sight of something important. Jesus says, "I must be about My Father's business." If they had known he must be about his Father's business, they would have known where to find him.

THE NECESSITY OF OUR EXISTENCE

Jesus kept in sight that which Mary and Joseph lost sight of. At the age of twelve he had a focus that he maintained. The mature Christian life is one that realizes the necessity of focus and of keeping focus. It is the life that avoids the pull of distraction and forgetfulness. In his statement, Jesus brings things back into focus for Mary and Joseph.

When Jesus says, "I must be about My Father's business," he reveals a consciousness about himself and a divine self-disclosure. He says, "I must be . . ." He does not say, "I might be." He says, "I *must* be." There is an awareness of the necessity of his being. It is a matter of must and not might. His being is not arbitrary or accidental. It is neither happenstance nor coincidence. His life is necessary. It is necessary that he be. It is necessary that he exist. It is necessary that he live.

To say "I must be" is to say: *I must keep the necessity of my existence in focus.*

The mature believer in Christ views his or her life from the standpoint of necessity. We understand that we are because it is necessary that we are. Our life is not optional or elective. Our life is necessary. Our life is essential. It is compulsory. There is an indispensable aspect to our being. We are here because it is necessary that we be here.

By reminding Mary of the necessity of his being, Jesus reminded Mary of her survival. The reason she escaped stoning for being pregnant before marriage was because Jesus must be. The reason they spent time in Egypt during the terror of Herod was because Jesus must be.

The necessity of our being helps explain the survival of our family line. The reason circumstances that could have destroyed our family line prior to our birth did not occur is because we must be. The reason our family story reads the way it does, and the reason certain events occurred, is because we must be. The reason certain sacrifices were made is because we must be. The reason certain threats were circumvented is because we must be. The reason certain attacks were short-circuited is because we must be. The reason the weapon formed against us did not prosper is because we must be.

You are here because you must be here. You exist because your existence is necessary for this time in the history of the world.

INTENTIONALITY OF LIFE

Jesus says, "I must be about." Jesus raises the issue of the "aboutness" of his life. His being is *about* something. There is an intention to his being. He's not here just to be here. There is a reason, a purpose, and an intention to his being.

To say "I must be about" is to say: *I must keep the intentionality of my life in focus.*

There is something about Jesus that causes Jesus to be. If we want to understand his being, we have to understand the intention behind, underneath, and within his being. His life is about something. It's not about nothing. There is rhyme and reason to his life. There is direction and aim to his life. There is a purpose toward which his life is drawn and lived. He must be about.

Necessary Christianity, maturity in Christ, ushers in recognition of the intentionality of life. We must be here because there is something our being here is about. The fact that we are alive and occupying space on earth is because our life is about something. There is an intention to our life and for our life. There is an intention that explains our life. There is an intention that challenges our life. Our being is not for nothing. Our being is for something. There's a reason we're here, why we are who we are. There's a reason we have the talents, gifts, and passions we do. There's also a reason we have the exposure and education we do. There's a reason we've had the opportunities we've had.

There is an aboutness to everything that concerns us. There's an intention to every aspect of our life, every circumstance that comes our way, every challenge we meet. Our life is about something every second, minute, hour, day, week, month, and year. In every encounter, our life is about something. In every engagement, our life is about something. In every experience, our life is about something.

Furthermore, to recognize the aboutness of our life is to resist the pull of negation. When challenges come our way, we have a tendency to view life from the standpoint of negation. We look at challenges in terms of their ability to negate us, to cause us to no longer be, to diminish who we are, or even to destroy us. The adversary paints a picture of negation. When we understand that our life is necessary and there is an intention that makes it necessary, we're able to look at any challenge and say that, even in the midst of it, our life is about something. It is the somethingness that will prevail. We will not recede into nothingness. The somethingness of our life demands that we survive. There is something God is doing in us and in what we're about.

This recognition of the intentionality of life not only tells us that our life is about something, it also informs us that our life should be about something. That is to say, we ought to be about something as we live our life. We ought to live every day being about something. There are many people living life about nothing. They're not about anything. They just are, but they aren't living about anything.

Others live about something, but not the something that their lives are intended to be about. Are we about what our life is about? Are we pursuing our life's intended purpose? Are we involved in what our life was intended to be involved in?

Necessary Christianity realizes there is a purpose for which we've been created. There is an aim and a goal we've been called to pursue. It is that purpose toward which our lives must be aimed.

Relationship with God

Jesus says, "I must be about My Father's . . ." To say this is to say: *To understand my purpose, I must keep my relationship with God in focus.*

Jesus finds the locus of intention for his life in a particular place. It is found in the context of his relationship with God the Father, who is the reason he exists in the world. God the Father is the reason he was born to Mary and Joseph. The intention of his being comes from God the Father. The intention for his being comes from God the Father. The aim of his earthly life is in God the Father. The direction toward which his life is lived is God the Father. He finds his reason for being through his relationship with God the Father.

Likewise, we discover what our lives are about through our relationship with God. We discover the true meaning and value of our life through the relationship we have with God. God is the reason we live and he is the person for whom we live.

God is the only way I can explain my continued existence. He is the reason I wake up in the morning. He is the reason I continue to breathe in and breathe out. In fact, it is in God I live, move, and have my being. He is the reason I'm still alive. He is the one for whom I live. My purpose is found in him. The rhyme and rhythm of my life is revealed by him. It is through him that I come to understand how the disparate pieces of my life fit together and see how the dots of my life are connected. It is through God that I come to understand the intentionality of my trials. I come to understand that "tribulation produces perseverance; perseverance, character; and character, hope. Now hope does not disappoint" (Romans 5:3-5). It's through God that I face affliction with intentionality, knowing that "our light affliction, which is but for a moment, is working for us a far more exceeding and eternal weight of glory" (2 Corinthians 4:17). It was through his relationship with God that Joseph found purpose and intentionality in his brothers' actions and was able to say, "But as for you, you meant evil against me; but God meant it for good, in order to bring it about as it is this day, to save many people alive" (Genesis 50:20).

Purpose is found in and through a relationship with God.

PURSUE YOUR CALLING

Jesus says, "I must be about My Father's business." In saying this, Jesus is emphasizing: *I must keep the calling that I am to pursue in focus.*

Mary says, "Son, why have you done this to us? Look, Your father and I have sought You anxiously." Jesus responds, "Why did you seek Me? Did you not know that I must be about My Father's business?" While Mary speaks of herself and Joseph, Jesus speaks of himself and God, of the necessity God has laid upon him. There is a necessity God has required of him. There is a necessity God has declared about him. It is that necessity about which he must direct his life. There is a calling upon him that he must pursue. There is business to which he must attend. It is his Father's business. He's not in the temple talking about a roofing contract or a furniture commission. That would have been talking about Joseph's business as a carpenter. He's there talking about the Scriptures, the Law and the Prophets. That's God the Father's business. There is a claim that God the Father has on Jesus' life that Jesus must pursue.

Jesus doesn't want Mary to be confused. The necessity of his life is not found in the carpentry business. The reason for his being in the world and the reason toward which his life is aimed is not construction. The reason for his life, the necessity of his life, lies not in his occupation but in his vocation. He must be about the Father's business and calling. He must be about what the Father has declared and demanded from his life. He must be about what the Father is laying upon his life.

Necessary Christianity is a maturity in Christ that knows the difference between occupation and vocation. It knows the difference between making a living and living the life God has called us to. While our life includes our occupation, it's more than our occupation. We are called to a vocation. We have a charge to keep. We live life knowing that the Father has some business for us to attend to. There's an assignment for our life, a calling on our life. God has requirements for our life. He has made a declaration about our life. We must be about our Father's business. We must be about the claim God has made on us. We must be found faithful in the stewardship with which we have been entrusted.

Jesus said, "Did you not know that I must be about My Father's business?" It's as though he was saying, "If you had remembered that I must be about my Father's business, you would have known where to find me. You would have known where to look for me. You would have known where I was. If you had remembered that I must be about my Father's business, you would have known to look for me in my Father's house first rather than last. You would have known that I'd be where the Father wanted me to be."

When we are about the Father's business, we are found where the Father is. We are found where the Father assigns us and where the Father has called us. There are some places where we must be found when we're about the Father's business. We must be found in the Father's house worshiping him and giving him glory. We must be found in the Father's house learning about him. We must be found in the midst of the fellowship of the saints of God. We must be found in the field being a witness for the Lord. We must be found on our knees praying to God. We must be found with our delight in the law of the Lord and on his law meditating day and night. When we live a necessary life, people should know where they can find us. They should know that they can find us pursuing the call of God.

2

I MUST PROGRESS

THE NECESSITY OF PROGRESSION

Now He arose from the synagogue and entered Simon's house. But Simon's wife's mother was sick with a high fever, and they made request of Him concerning her. So He stood over her and rebuked the fever, and it left her. And immediately she arose and served them.

When the sun was setting, all those who had any that were sick with various diseases brought them to Him; and He laid His hands on every one of them and healed them. And demons also came out of many, crying out and saying, "You are the Christ, the Son of God!"

And He, rebuking them, did not allow them to speak, for they knew that He was the Christ.

Now when it was day, He departed and went into a deserted place. And the crowd sought Him and came to Him, and tried to keep Him from leaving them; but He said to them, "I must preach the kingdom of God to the other cities also, because for this purpose I have been sent." And He was preaching in the synagogues of Galilee. (Luke 4:38-44)

I n the preceding chapter, we discovered that a life with God in Christ Jesus requires some things of us that are not optional but obligatory. The life of Jesus as revealed in the Gospels is a life lived under necessity, by necessity, and with necessity. As early as age twelve Jesus exhibited a life oriented around "mustness" and not "mightness." He displayed a necessity of focus that recognized the necessity of his existence, the intentionality of his life, his purpose being connected to his relationship with God the Father, and his having a calling to pursue.

Jesus is now an adult, about thirty years of age. It is the morning of his ministry. The experience of the heavens opening over the baptismal waters of the Jordan River, with the Spirit of God descending on him in the form of a dove and the voice of God the Father declaring, "This is My Beloved Son, in whom I am well pleased" (Matthew 3:17), is still fresh upon him. Even fresher is the experience of demonic temptation in the wilderness after forty days and forty nights of fasting and praying, as well as his being rejected by people from his own hometown.

Jesus is now in Capernaum. He has spent one day ministering in the synagogue, casting out a demon in one man, healing Peter's mother-in-law of her fever, and healing others and driving out other demons from people who crowded the house of Peter's in-laws. Having rested the night, Jesus awakens early in the morning and goes to a deserted place to spend time alone with God. He needs to be refreshed, renewed, and revived. The crowd that came to Peter's in-laws' home searches for Jesus and finds him. They try to contain him. They urge him to remain where he is with them. Jesus responds to them saying, "I must preach the kingdom of God to the other cities also, because for this purpose I have been sent."

Jesus has encountered early success in his ministry. Capernaum has been a good place for him. He has healed the sick and driven out demons. There is no opposition to what he's doing. The crowds grow increasingly larger. The people are coming after him. They are leaving the city and coming out into the desert. Jesus could do well for himself in Capernaum. The people want him to stay.

Who could ask for anything better? What more could you want than to be in a successful place with a locked-in market that is ever increasing? People work all their lives to get to that place. Jesus is in this position in the morning of his ministry. But with this one city begging him to stay, Jesus says, "I must preach the kingdom of God to the other cities also, because for this purpose I have been sent."

Jesus makes this statement out of an understanding of the nature of the life to which he is called. It is a life of progression. The people are suggesting that Jesus settle down and stay where he is currently. Demand for him is growing in Capernaum. He is experiencing increasing popularity. While his own people in Nazareth rejected him and sought to throw him over a cliff, the people in Capernaum celebrate him. Who wouldn't be able to get used to that? Who wouldn't be satisfied with that?

Jesus understands that while he could settle in Capernaum, the claim of God on his life demands something else. It demands that he withstand the pull of being satisfied where he is. He must resist the temptation to remain in one place. He cannot stay where he is because his life and calling are dynamic. His life is one that must move forward.

The life of the Christian is fraught with occasions where the crowds say to us, "Stay right here." The temptation is to remain static. It is to localize ourselves within one point in time and space. It is to be satisfied with where we are and who we are, such that we don't move any further forward in life.

This temptation resonates with us on a variety of levels. It hits us on the level of our minds. We are tempted to be satisfied with the current way we think. We are content with our thoughts. We don't need any new ideas. We don't need any new mental challenges. We don't need any different concepts or approaches. After all, we've done pretty well with the approaches and concepts we already have. Why rock the boat? Why mess with a good thing? If it isn't broken, don't fix it.

We also deal with this temptation physically. We become attached to a place. We like where we are. We like our seat. We like our area. We like our position. Things are going well where we are. The Lord is blessing us where we are. There's no need to move away. We've gotten accustomed to being in this place. The drive isn't bad where we are. We know everybody and everybody knows us.

The temptation to be static affects us relationally as well. We have a nice group of people around us. We don't need to add anybody else. We have a good routine with the people we know. We don't need to change it. We're comfortable with these folks. We're safe as we are. It's predictable. Let's not go upsetting the apple cart.

THE DYNAMIC NATURE OF LIFE IN CHRIST

Let's admit that most of us prefer predictability. Living a static life is appealing. Jesus understood that his life was not meant to be static. It was meant to be dynamic and progressive. Through this episode in Jesus' life, we learn that we must live lives that are dynamically progressive. This forces us to acknowledge: *I must accept the dynamic nature of life in Christ.*

For the disciple of Jesus Christ, life is not static; it is dynamic. As a matter of fact, life itself is by nature not static but dynamic. It is not one big moment but a series of moments, each proceeding from the other. God is not a static God. He is dynamic. For example, God is dynamic in his work in the world. God is constantly moving and acting within the world. God is dynamic in his self-revelation. He does not reveal himself or his plan in a singular moment. He does it progressively because we can't handle it all at once. We aren't ready for everything in one moment. God uses a series of moments that build on each other to create understanding, to establish momentum, to build strength, and to develop faith for what is to come. That's why the mature Christian can confidently say, "The best is yet to come." Whatever God has done in, for, with, and through our life is not so we can become self-satisfied and stuck but so we can be strengthened and readied for what is ahead.

Jesus understood that the lines of his life were not static but dynamic. There was more for him to do in more places. There were more people for him to bless. There was more territory to take from the devil.

His purpose could not be fulfilled if he remained where he was. He had to move. He had to go further. The purpose of God always demands progressive movement. It requires action. This is not movement simply for its own sake. It's movement for the sake of progress. It's action that has advancement in mind. The people were thinking about maintaining and localizing Jesus and the power of the kingdom. However, Jesus understood that the plan of God was for the kingdom to advance. It was that the power of God be expanded in the earth. It was that the good news of the gospel be extended to all people. Though it would start out minuscule and in relative obscurity, the kingdom would flourish and spread like a mustard seed that grows into the largest of shrubs. So the expansion and the extension of the kingdom of God demanded that Jesus go beyond Capernaum.

Likewise, for the mature Christian, the purpose of God for our life and service is not one of maintenance and localization. It is one of expansion and extension. God seeks to show himself to us and through us in ever-increasing depth and dimension. God seeks to expand his influence by providing us with expanded opportunities to be and to do. There are other realms where he wants to be known through us. There are other dimensions where he wants to be seen in us. There are other circles where he wants to be felt through us. There are other spheres where God wants to be recognized through us.

Living by Assignment

Jesus says, "I must preach the kingdom of God to the other cities also, because for this purpose I have been sent." This not only causes us to acknowledge the dynamic nature of life, but also it causes us to acknowledge: *My life must be lived by assignment and not by preference.*

Jesus' statement to the crowd is not about his preference. He does not talk about what he'd like to do. He talks about what he must do. His life is lived from the understanding that he's been sent. The Greek word for "send" is *apostellō*, from which we get the derivative "apostle." It means to go to an appointed place. Jesus speaks of his existence from the standpoint of being sent, assigned, appointed. He is under orders. He is about the Father's business. As one who is about the Father's business, he doesn't live his life according to preference. He lives according to assignment and appointment. While it would have been nice to remain in Capernaum, his assignment extends beyond its limits. While everybody likes him in Capernaum, his directive is to go to other places where not everybody will like him. While the people's faith is great and conducive to miracles in Capernaum, Jesus' purpose is to go to places where faith is not as great.

There is a perspective that sees life as being simply about us. It's about what we want, what we desire, and what we dream. That view is preferable to most people, including Christians. The problem is that such a view is not Christian. The life of the believer is not about what the believer wants. It's about what God wants for the believer. It's about what God desires for us and from us. It's about the lines God has drawn for our life. It's about what God has appointed and assigned.

The tension we experience in life is often due to the fact that there is distance and dissonance between our preference and God's assignment. We prefer a path of certainty and predictability, and God appoints us to a walk of faith and by faith. We prefer to live lives of acquisition and accumulation, and God assigns us to live lives of stewardship, savings, and sacrificial giving. We prefer to persist in the tried and true, and God assigns us to pursue what's never been attempted.

The life of the Christian is to be lived from the perspective of assignment and not preference. In fact, we demonstrate maturity in Christ when we are able to make God's assignment our preference. Hear Jesus say in John 4:34, "My food is to do the will of Him who sent Me, and to finish His work." He says in John 5:19-20, "The Son can do nothing of Himself, but what He sees the Father do; for whatever He does, the Son also does in like manner. For the Father loves the Son, and shows Him all things that He Himself does." Maturity in Christ is seeing the Father's appointments and assignments and making them our preference. Maturity in Christ recognizes the dynamic nature of life in Christ.

The dynamic nature of life in Christ partly results from the way God's appointments and assignments precede our arrival. God isn't making up our life as we go. God has drawn the lines of our life. He has established the path and terrain of our life. There are certain appointments and assignments God has for our life that we haven't even dreamed or imagined.

Eye has not seen, nor ear heard,
Nor have entered into the heart of man
The things which God has prepared for those who
    love Him. (1 Corinthians 2:9)

There are assignments and appointments ahead of us. They require that we refuse to get stuck and complacent. The assigned life frees us for what is yet ahead. Life under divine assignment and appointment recognizes that no point or place in life can be called absolute. No point or place in life can be claimed as the place where we just settle. As long as we live, God has assignments and appointments with our name on them. They require us to move. They require us to stretch. They require us to grow. They require us to extend ourselves beyond the place where we are mentally, emotionally, spiritually, relationally, occupationally, vocationally, and physically. We can never be too old, too established, too settled. God can call our name at the age of seventy-five, as he did with Abraham, and assign us to go to a land he will show us.

The mature Christian lives from the perspective of assignment and not preference. Sometimes when we will not free ourselves from preference to pursue appointment and assignment, God allows circumstances to free us. Remember the story of Jonah? God gave Jonah an assignment that wasn't Jonah's preference. Jonah tried to avoid the assignment and hold on to his preference by boarding a ship headed in the opposite direction from the assignment. God sent a storm over the sea that resulted in Jonah being thrown overboard. God then sent a great fish that swallowed Jonah, in whose belly Jonah remained for three days and three nights. When Jonah released his hold on his preference and cried out to the Lord, the Lord ordered the fish to spit Jonah out. God spoke his assignment to Jonah a second time. That time, Jonah walked in the assignment of God.

You may recall a time when you wouldn't free yourself from your preference to accept God's appointment and assignment for your life, so God allowed circumstances to come your way that freed you from yourself. Since you wouldn't let it go, God let it let go for you.

In some cases, during times of upheaval, God is freeing us from our preference so we can pursue his appointment and assignment for our life. We won't voluntarily leave comfort, convenience, or false security to pursue purpose and find destiny, so God allows a storm to come our way to get us out of the boat. The good news of the story is that if God has sent a storm to get us out of the boat to be free for what he has for us, God will not let us drown in the water. God has an appointment and an assignment. We may have to tread water for a while. We may even spend some time in what seems to be confinement like the belly of a great fish. But we will not drown. We will not die. We will live. God has us under orders. God has appointments and assignments.

Continuity Regardless of Context

Jesus says, "I must preach the kingdom of God to the other cities also, because for this purpose I have been sent." Luke 4:44 reads, "So he continued to travel around, preaching in synagogues throughout Judea" (NLT). Besides acknowledging that we must live a dynamically progressive life and live by assignment and not by preference, there is a third acknowledgment we must make: *I must live from the standpoint of continuity, regardless of my context.*

With the people of Capernaum, in Galilee, begging Jesus to remain with them, Jesus lets them know he must preach the gospel in other towns also, because that is why he was sent. The next verse says he continued traveling around and preaching in the synagogues throughout Judea. He continued with the assignment. He kept moving. He kept traveling. Everywhere he went, he preached the gospel.

Luke emphasizes that Jesus is preaching in the synagogues throughout Judea. There are two possible meanings of this passage. The first meaning is the southern province of Israel being Judea. The story of our text takes place in the city of Capernaum, in the province of Galilee. Galilee is the northern province of Israel, with Capernaum in the middle, and Judea is the southern province. It's between fifty and sixty miles on foot or donkey from Capernaum in Galilee to towns in Judea. It's an arduous journey through desert places and mountainous regions—yet Jesus continued. The people in the provinces in Judea were of a different background than those of Galilee. They tended to look on Galileans as uncultured, unlettered, and less spiritual. Yet Jesus continued preaching the gospel because he was under assignment in Judea. The Judeans may have viewed him with suspicion. They may have looked down on him. They may have discounted his message. Yet he continued preaching and serving under the assignment.

The second usage of "Judea" is in a general sense, referring to the whole commonwealth of Israel, which includes but is not limited to Judea. It consists of Galilee, Samaria, Decapolis, Idumea, and Tyre. It means regardless of the context, Jesus continued. Whether in favorable or hostile territory, Jesus continued. Whether among friends or enemies, Jesus continued.

The mature Christian who lives life under appointment and assignment does not shrink when the appointment or assignment occurs in a less-than-ideal context. The mature Christian does not get hung up on the context of the assignment. The mature Christian does not get bogged down by the circumstantial conditions around the assignment. The mature Christian knows that he or she is under orders. The mature Christian knows that his or her steps are ordered by the Lord and the Lord delights in the way of the believer. The mature Christian knows that continuity is not based on the consistency of the situation. It's based on the consistency of the Father. He is the same yesterday, today, and forever (Hebrews 13:8).

Jesus continued preaching the gospel regardless of context because the Father was the same. The assignment did not change. The importance did not change. The power did not change. The anointing did not change. He continued. God's purpose for his life and God's call on his life kept him moving. His life was dynamic. Jesus overcame the temptation to settle.

Look at Jesus in heavenly glory on the Mount of Transfiguration with Moses on one side and Elijah on the other. Peter says, "It is good for us to be here; and let us make three tabernacles: one for You, one for Moses, and one for Elijah" (Mark 9:5). Peter was saying, "Let's just settle down here on this mountain." Nevertheless, Jesus continued. He ignored what was implied in the comment. He left the mountain because there was more assigned to him. There were appointments ahead for him. A father whose son was vexed by a dumb spirit. Children brought by their parents. A rich young ruler. Blind Bartimaeus. Zacchaeus. Mary, Martha, and Lazarus. Calvary.

In the Garden of Gethsemane, there is Jesus' preference and there is God's assignment. Jesus' preference is to avoid the cup. His desire is for the cup to pass from him. But because he is on assignment, he doesn't stop with his preference. He ends his prayer, "Nevertheless not My will, but Yours, be done" (Luke 22:42). Jesus continues his assignment on Calvary's mountain. Jesus fulfills his assignment to die for our sins. Jesus accomplishes his assignment by shedding his blood. Jesus fulfills his assignment by dying on the cross. He does so because he knows that not only is he appointed to die; he is appointed to be raised. God the Father will keep his appointment, and in fact, early Sunday morning, God kept his appointment and raised Jesus from the dead.

The mature Christian revels in the fact that Jesus didn't stop.

3

I MUST BE DIRECTED

THE NECESSITY OF DIRECTION

Therefore, when the Lord knew that the Pharisees had heard that Jesus made and baptized more disciples than John (though Jesus Himself did not baptize, but His disciples), He left Judea and departed again to Galilee. But He needed to go through Samaria.

So He came to a city of Samaria which is called Sychar, near the plot of ground that Jacob gave to his son Joseph. Now Jacob's well was there. Jesus therefore, being wearied from His journey, sat thus by the well. It was about the sixth hour.

A woman of Samaria came to draw water. Jesus said to her, "Give Me a drink." For His disciples had gone away into the city to buy food.

Then the woman of Samaria said to Him, "How is it that You, being a Jew, ask a drink from me, a Samaritan woman?" For Jews have no dealings with Samaritans.

Jesus answered and said to her, "If you knew the gift of God, and who it is who says to you, 'Give Me a drink,' you would have asked Him, and He would have given you living water."

The woman said to Him, "Sir, You have nothing to draw with, and the well is deep. Where then do You get that living water? Are You greater than our father Jacob, who gave us the well, and drank from it himself, as well as his sons and his livestock?"

Jesus answered and said to her, "Whoever drinks of this water will thirst again, but whoever drinks of the water that I shall give him will never thirst. But the water that I shall give him will become in him a fountain of water springing up into everlasting life."

The woman said to Him, "Sir, give me this water, that I may not thirst, nor come here to draw."

Jesus said to her, "Go, call your husband, and come here."

The woman answered and said, "I have no husband."

Jesus said to her, "You have well said, 'I have no husband,' for you have had five husbands, and the one whom you now have is not your husband; in that you spoke truly."

The woman said to Him, "Sir, I perceive that You are a prophet. Our fathers worshiped on this mountain and you Jews say that in Jerusalem is the place where one ought to worship."

Jesus said to her, "Woman, believe Me, the hour is coming when you will neither on this mountain, nor in Jerusalem, worship the Father. You worship what you do not know; we know what we worship, for salvation is of the Jews. But the hour is coming, and now is, when the true worshipers will worship the Father in spirit and truth; for the Father is seeking such to worship Him. God is Spirit and those who worship Him must worship in spirit and truth."

The woman said to Him, "I know that Messiah is coming" (who is called Christ). "When He comes, He will tell us all things."

Jesus said to her, "I who speak to you am He."

And at this point His disciples came, and they marveled that He talked with a woman; yet no one said, "What do You seek?" or, "Why are You talking with her?"

The woman then left her waterpot, went her way into the city, and said to the men, "Come, see a Man who told me all things that I ever did. Could this be the Christ?" Then they went out of the city and came to Him. (John 4:1-30)

T he mature Christian comes to understand that some things are simply necessary. They are without compromise. They are essential. It is essential for the Christian to maintain focus and a sense of dynamic progression. The cause of Christ is focused and dynamic in nature.

It must be said that this dynamism is not random. The Christian is not called to action that is arbitrary or erratic. The life of the Christian is lived neither by chance nor by accident. The mature Christian is one who lives his or her life under the direction of God. It is the Christian's pleasure to have his or her steps ordered by the Lord. The psalmist tells us that

The steps of a good man are ordered by the LORD,
And He delights in His way. (Psalm 37:23)

The writer of Proverbs admonishes us to

> Trust in the LORD with all your heart,
> And lean not on your own understanding;
> In all your ways acknowledge Him,
> And He shall direct your paths. (Proverbs 3:5-6)

The life of the believer in Christ is to be lived following the voice of God in the direction that God reveals.

The direction of God is not a suggestion. It's not an implication, hint, or tip, but a command. It is an authoritative instruction. God directs and guides us based on his purpose and plan for our lives and for the world. At every point when God speaks a word of direction, it is a necessary word for that point in time. When he issues it, we must know that it is necessary that we follow it.

Of course, for many of us, the problem is when God leads us in a way that doesn't fit with our agenda or our sense of propriety. Yet the life of Jesus informs us that even when God directs in an inconvenient or unconventional way, we must view it and our walking in it as necessary.

Nowhere is this more clearly seen than in John 4. Jesus has been ministering in Jerusalem and in the province of Judea. He has held night sessions with a Pharisee named Nicodemus and explained both the necessity and the means of the new birth. The word among the Pharisees is that Jesus is a greater threat than John. Upon realizing this, Jesus knows that his time in Judea is coming to an end. He will go back to Galilee. The next verse reads, "But He needed to go through Samaria."

While the most direct route from Judea in the south to Galilee in the north is through Samaria, most Jews would go around Samaria rather than through it. They did so because of the historical animosity between them and the Samaritans. This hostility dated back to the time of the Assyrian invasion of Israel and the subsequent intermarrying of Jews and Assyrians, which resulted in persons of mixed blood—an affront to the traditional Jewish sensibility. These Jews who intermarried were called Samaritans as a pejorative. They were denied the opportunity to assist in the rebuilding of the temple in Jerusalem during the time of Ezra. They also were denied access to worship in the temple in Jerusalem. Hence the common practice of Jews traveling from Judea to Galilee was to go around Samaria.

With this in mind, we can't help but be struck by the statement concerning Jesus' itinerary. "He needed to go through Samaria." This is not said of Jesus in John 2:13 when Jesus left Galilee to go to Judea. There is no mention of his traveling through Samaria. Therefore we may assume that he went around it. Yet in Jesus' return to Galilee, John alerts us that Jesus "needed to go through Samaria."

Jesus is under the direction of God. And God has revealed to him the necessity of traveling through Samaria.

GO TO PLACES OTHERS AVOID

When we look at this verse and the story that follows, we come to see some things about God's direction and the necessity of our following it. Seeing them causes us to acknowledge this reality: *I must follow God's direction to places others would avoid.*

While it was the practice of the Jews to avoid Samaria, God directs Jesus to enter into it. What is of particular interest is that God allowed Jesus to avoid Samaria before. While Jesus was allowed to skirt around the region before, this time he must go through it. He must enter into Samaria. He cannot avoid it.

Mature Christian living entails understanding that God at times directs us to places and positions others avoid. He may even direct us to a place, situation, or position that we ourselves once avoided. There may have been a time when God allowed us to ignore it or go around it, but then God called us to go into it. He called us to go through it. He called us to take it head-on.

Jesus must go through Samaria because it is a part of God's itinerary for his life. For whom God was calling Jesus to be at that point in time, Samaria was necessary. For what God wanted to do through Jesus and with Jesus at that time, Samaria was necessary. Some things are necessary because of whom God is trying to make us to be and what God is trying to accomplish in and through our lives. While God may allow others to avoid it, he doesn't allow us to avoid it because the particular itinerary of our life demands that we go through. It demands that we enter. It requires that we face.

Necessary Christianity understands that there are parts of the divinely navigated path through which we must go. No bit of fasting will change it. No length of prayer will change it. We must go through it.

ENGAGE THOSE WHOM OTHERS SHUN

Jesus and the disciples enter Samaria and arrive at a city called Sychar, which is near the land Jacob gave to Joseph. It is an area filled with memory for the Jewish people. It was formerly known as Shechem. This was where the bones of Joseph were buried after they were brought up from Egypt. It was at this place that Joshua assembled the people before his death, and it was here where they renewed their covenant with the Lord (Joshua 24:32). Jesus approaches a well named Jacob's well. The tradition was that Jacob dug the well.

Meanwhile, the disciples go into town to buy food. As Jesus sits at the well, a woman approaches to draw water. It is an unusual time for drawing water; it is high noon. The woman is drawing water at this hour to avoid the negative attention of the townspeople. Some readers and scholars suggest that she was a woman of bad reputation. As she draws water, Jesus asks her to give him a drink. The woman responds, "How is it that You, being a Jew, ask a drink from me, a Samaritan woman?" John reminds us parenthetically that the Jews have no dealings with Samaritans.

It is here that the second acknowledgment arises: *I must follow God's direction to engage those whom others would shun.*

The woman is shocked that Jesus is speaking to her. After all, he is a Jewish male and she is a Samaritan woman. It is inappropriate for him to speak to her for two reasons. First of all, rabbinic law forbade a Jewish male, especially a rabbi, from openly speaking to a woman. One rule, noted in John Gill's *Exposition on the Bible*, reads, "Do not multiply discourse with a woman, with his wife they say, much less with his neighbor's wife: hence the wise men say, at whatsoever time a man multiplies discourse with a woman, he is the cause of evil to himself, and ceases from the words of the law, and at last shall go down into hell." This was even more the case in a public setting. Another rule reads, "Let not a man talk with a woman in the streets, even with his wife; and there is no need to say with another man's wife."

The second reason the conversation is inappropriate is that the woman is a Samaritan. The acrimony and antipathy between their two people groups forbids such interaction. No respectable Jewish male would be seen speaking to a Samaritan woman. Furthermore, because of her alleged reputation, no male would be seen speaking to her in public. Many may have spoken to her in private, but there was probably no man in that region who would speak with her openly for fear of how he might be seen.

None of this fazes Jesus. He openly and directly engages this woman in conversation. He does so because necessity and purpose are connected to this engagement. It is not by accident that he is at the well at high noon. The God who ordered his steps knew the woman would be traveling to the well at that same time. God intended this interaction to happen. God plotted this intersection. Jesus must engage this woman because the purpose of God demands it.

God will direct us to engage people others would shun. God will bring us across the path of people in whom others take little or no interest. God brings us across their path and them across our path because there is a word he wants to speak to them through us. There is a message God wants to deliver to them through us. There is a smile, a handshake, or even a hug God wants to extend to them through us. While others may be afraid of them or ashamed to be identified with them, God directs you and me to engage them. God directs us to engage the homeless person, the HIV/AIDS patient, the recently released convicted felon, the person fighting addiction, the child with the behavior problem, and so on.

God will bring us to them and them to us at a critical point. In that moment God will give us a directive. It may be something as simple as directing us to smile and look them in the eyes. It may be to provide a word of encouragement or pray with them. It may be to offer them a meal or connect them with a prospective employer. When God does so, there is urgency to it. It is a weighty matter, not just in terms of what God provides the person, but also in terms of whom God is making us to become.

Every time God directs us to engage those whom others would shun, he is working on an aspect of our own character. He's developing our ability to hear him and respond to him. He's increasing our obedience. He's enlarging our heart for him and for others. He's improving our servant spirit and heart. He's causing us to reexamine our assumptions and perceptions. He's developing within us less of a worry about what people will think of us, because our concern is how we look in God's eyes and not how we look in people's eyes.

God directs us to engage those whom others shun. What a lesson this is, especially for young people. If we are able to ingrain this in the minds of Christian young people, we will avoid some teenage suicides and rebellious behavior. Christian young people must know that God calls and directs them to engage people whom others shun. God calls young people to engage those whom others deem uncool. God calls us to reject the pull to join the crowd in bullying, shunning, teasing, harassing, and isolating those not as popular as the rest. It is those very people God will direct us to befriend. God will direct us to eat at the lunch table where they're eating. God will direct us to publicly affirm them.

The truth is that we never know how much our words mean to them. We can't imagine how much our smile means to them. We can't fathom how valuable it is to sit at the lunch table with them or allow them to sit at the lunch table with us. In those instances when God speaks directly to us and guides us to engage the unpopular, it is a necessary engagement. God may use our kindness to cause them to believe that life matters. God may use our example to spur them on to view life with hope.

Jesus engages the woman in dialogue designed to bring her to terms with herself and her need for Jesus. He's not talking to her just to shoot the breeze. There is an aim to this conversation. There is purpose to this discussion. The ultimate end of this engagement is for Jesus to reveal himself to her as Messiah. When God directs us into a space or a position, we must realize that some degree of revelation is attached to it. There is something God desires to reveal to those with whom we come into contact. The greatest revelation God can give is the revelation of his love for others in Christ Jesus.

FOLLOW GOD INTO WHAT OTHERS DON'T UNDERSTAND

Jesus carefully leads this woman into the truth about her condition, her need, and his ability to meet the need. In

John 4:25 the woman reveals, "'I know that Messiah is coming' (who is called Christ). 'When He comes, He will tell us all things.'" Jesus responds, "I who speak to you am He."

At this point the disciples approach. They can't believe their eyes. Jesus is speaking to a woman out in public! What's more, this woman is a Samaritan! The sun must have gotten to Jesus. Jesus has forgotten who he is and where he is. This is the way it appears to the disciples.

It is here that Jesus reveals the third acknowledgment: *I must follow God's direction into that which is greater than what others can see or understand.*

The disciples look at Jesus talking to this woman from the perspective of convention. Here is a Jewish rabbi talking to a Samaritan woman in broad daylight. The common practice among the rabbinic order was that even if a man met his wife on the street, he would not speak to her so as to maintain the appearance of chastity and temperance. Yet here is Jesus talking to this woman. The disciples would see only the narrow event of Jesus speaking with the Samaritan woman. They didn't know there was more to this than what they saw.

Jesus alludes to this when he tells them in John 4:32-35, "I have food to eat of which you do not know. . . . My food is to do the will of Him who sent Me, and to finish His work. Do you not say, 'There are still four months and then comes the harvest'? Behold, I say to you, lift up your eyes and look at the fields, for they are already white for harvest!"

With the disciples looking at the situation narrowly, Jesus expands their understanding by showing them that this whole episode is under the direction of God. God's direction has a much broader reality in mind. While the disciples can see only the woman to whom Jesus is talking, God sees the city the woman will influence. Their journey through Samaria, Jesus resting at the well, the woman coming out to the well to draw water at the time when Jesus was there, and Jesus' conversation with the woman have to do with much more than the woman herself. They have to do with the city of Sychar. There is a harvest of souls whose reaping God has timed with their trip through Samaria and with Jesus' conversation with the woman. God has seen the impact of Jesus' conversation with the woman ahead of time. He knows the woman is ripe for the conversation. She is ready for a change in her life. The readiness and ripeness of the woman reflect the condition of the whole city. If God can get to the woman, the woman can get to the city.

As Jesus speaks to the disciples about the harvest before them, the people of the city walk toward the well. Despite the woman's possibly unsavory reputation, the people of the city hear her testimony, "Come see a man who told me everything I ever did. Could this be the

Christ?" In fact, many believe in Jesus because of the woman's testimony.

God's directions are according to God's purpose and God's plan. God's purpose and plan are always beyond what is conceivable to the human mind. Truly:

> Eye has not seen, nor ear heard,
> Nor have entered into the heart of man
> The things which God has prepared for those who
>   love Him. (1 Corinthians 2:9)

Also:

> "My thoughts are not your thoughts,
> Nor are your ways My ways," says the LORD.
> "For as the heavens are higher than the earth,
> So are My ways higher than your ways,
> And My thoughts than your thoughts."
>   (Isaiah 55:8-9)

When God directs us into the unconventional, the unusual, the unfamiliar, and the uncommon, we must know that God has more in mind than others can see.

When God directs us in this way, we can know we are in good company. Moses will tell us that God leads us into the unconventional and unusual. He tells Moses to lead the people in the direction of the Red Sea. Moses does so. This journey places the people in an uneasy and inconvenient position. Pharaoh's army is behind them. Wilderness and mountain ranges are beside them. The Red

Sea is in front of them. On the surface, this makes no sense. All the people can see is their destruction. But God sees their deliverance and the defeat of the Egyptian hosts. God has Moses tell the people, "Stand still, and see the salvation of the LORD, which He will accomplish for you today. For the Egyptians whom you see today, you shall see again no more forever" (Exodus 14:13). God had more in mind than what the people could see.

Joshua will tell us that God directed him and the people to march around the walls of Jericho for seven days. On the seventh day, they were to march around seven times. On the seventh time, they were to shout. This was an unconventional direction. To many, all they could see were people marching around walls that were still standing. But God had more in mind. On the seventh day at the seventh time, when the people shouted, the walls came tumbling down. God's directions have more in mind than others can see.

God directs Jesus to freely give himself to Judas and the mob. He directs Jesus to humbly go with the mob and stand before the Sanhedrin council. He directs Jesus to refuse to mount a defense. To the casual observer, it seems as if Jesus is resigned to death and defeat. It appears as if Jesus has thrown in the towel. As they hang him on the cross between two thieves, it appears as if Jesus is done. As Jesus breathes his last breath, his enemies claim the victory. Jesus is crucified. He's now dead.

But they don't know that in Jesus' crucifixion and death, God has more in mind than they can see. God has the fulfillment of Isaiah's prophecy in mind. God has the redemption of souls in mind. Jesus tried to warn them when he said, "I, if I am lifted up from the earth, will draw all peoples to Myself" (John 12:32). God has the defeat of Satan in mind. God has the vanquishing of hell in mind. God has victory over death and the grave in mind. God has your and my salvation in mind.

It was necessary that Jesus not just go through Samaria, but also that he go through the cross at Calvary, through dying, through burial, through hell, and early on the third day, that God raise him up with all power in his hand. It was necessary that he go back to heaven, through the Most Holy Place, and sprinkle his blood there for us all.

Through Jesus, I've learned that some places are necessary for me to go through. Some battles are necessary for me to fight. Some burdens are necessary for me to carry, and some experiences are necessary for me to have. My sentiment now is, "If Jesus leads me, I'll go." Where he leads me, I will follow. It may be inconvenient, unpopular, and unconventional, but I still will follow. I must be directed, and in being directed, it is necessary for me to follow.

4

I MUST BE CLEAR

THE NECESSITY OF CLARITY

When Jesus came into the region of Caesarea Philippi, He asked His disciples, saying, "Who do men say that I, the Son of Man, am?"

So they said, "Some say John the Baptist, some Elijah, and others Jeremiah or one of the prophets."

He said to them, "But who do you say that I am?"

Simon Peter answered and said, "You are the Christ, the Son of the living God."

Jesus answered and said to him, "Blessed are you, Simon Bar-Jonah, for flesh and blood has not revealed this to you, but My Father who is in heaven. And I also say to you that you are Peter, and on this rock I will build My church, and the gates of Hades shall not prevail against it. And I will give you the keys of the kingdom of heaven, and whatever you bind on earth will be bound in heaven, and whatever you loose on earth will be loosed in heaven."

Then He commanded His disciples that they should tell no one that He was Jesus the Christ.

> From that time Jesus began to show to His disciples
> that He must go to Jerusalem, and suffer many things
> from the elders and chief priests and scribes, and be
> killed, and be raised the third day.
>
> Then Peter took Him aside and began to rebuke Him,
> saying, "Far be it from You, Lord; this shall not happen
> to You!"
>
> But He turned and said to Peter, "Get behind Me,
> Satan! You are an offense to Me, for you are not mindful
> of the things of God, but the things of men."
>
> Then Jesus said to His disciples, "If anyone desires to
> come after Me, let him deny himself, and take up his
> cross, and follow Me. For whoever desires to save his life
> will lose it, but whoever loses his life for My sake will find
> it. For what profit is it to a man if he gains the whole
> world, and loses his own soul? Or what will a man give in
> exchange for his soul? For the Son of Man will come in
> the glory of His Father with His angels, and then He will
> reward each according to his works. (Matthew 16:13-27)

As we have examined the "must" statements of Jesus and about Jesus, we have learned some things about the necessary life to which we are called. We have learned that we must live God-focused lives. We must live dynamically progressive and God-directed lives.

The text before us reveals another necessary characteristic of the Christian life. Jesus and the disciples are in Caesarea Philippi. Against the backdrop of Mt. Hermon,

Jesus raises two questions to his group. The first is, "Who do men say that I, the Son of Man, am?" The second is, "Who do you say that I am?"

They respond to the first question with John the Baptist, Elijah, Jeremiah, or one of the other prophets. Peter answers the second by saying, "You are the Christ, the Son of the living God." Jesus informs Peter that his answer is not the result of flesh and blood. It is the result of revelation from God the Father. The revelation of Jesus being the Christ will be the rock, the foundation, upon which the church will be built and against which the gates of hell will not prevail. Jesus also entrusts Peter with the keys of the kingdom of heaven and invests within him the power of binding and loosing. Jesus then warns them not to tell anyone he is the Christ.

It is here that we receive our textual verses, which read, "From that time Jesus began to show to His disciples that He must go to Jerusalem, and suffer many things from the elders and chief priests and scribes, and be killed, and be raised the third day."

With Peter's declaration of Jesus being the Christ, Jesus begins to explain what that means. Jesus is aware of the popular notion and expectation concerning the Christ or the Messiah among the Jews. Many held an image of an earthly king who would liberate the people from the tyranny of Rome and reestablish the kingdom of Israel as remembered during the reign of David. Jesus also knows that who he is and what he has been sent to do as the Christ differ from what most expect. With Peter and the other disciples having a different idea about his person and his assignment, Jesus clarifies who he is as the Christ. Furthermore, he clarifies what they should expect as a result of who he is.

In so doing, Jesus reveals another aspect of the mature Christian: *The mature Christian must be clear about who she is and what she is called to do.*

The direction God gives is designed to provide clarity. However, in order for us to possess the clarity God desires, we must first accept what God speaks and then assert what God speaks.

ACCEPT THE REALITY OF SUFFERING

Jesus offers clarification to Peter and the others based on what he knows and has accepted. He reveals that life in him is a life that seeks to declare: *I must accept and assert the reality of sacrifice and suffering as part of the walk with Christ.*

Given the popular notion of the Christ as an earthly liberator-king who would vanquish the forces of Rome and usher in a return to the glorious Davidic era, Jesus clearly explains that he must suffer many things at the hands of the elders, chief priests, and teachers of the law and that he must be killed. Jesus presents a different image of the Messiah-Christ that does not fit the role of the Messiah as king, prophet, and priest. The image of the Messiah-Christ he presents is the image of sacrifice and suffering.

There are many who desire to wish away any sense of sacrifice or suffering from the Christian faith. They believe that if they can simply avoid uttering words about sickness, disease, and so forth, they can avoid experiencing those realities. For them, faith is a prophylactic that shields them from discomfort and pain. For them, faith is about conquest, victory, being above, and being over. After all, who doesn't like conquest, victory, being above, and being on top? All of us prefer that state of affairs.

However, the Christian life is not all conquest. It's not all victory. It's not all being above and on top. Some of us experience defeat, disappointment, being behind, being beneath, and being under. We experience persecution, attack, and isolation. In Hebrews 11, the account of a great cascade of heroes and heroines of faith reaches its apex in verse 33:

> Through faith [they] subdued kingdoms, worked righteousness, obtained promises, stopped the mouths of lions, quenched the violence of fire, escaped the edge of the sword, out of weakness were made strong, became valiant in battle, turned to flight the armies of the aliens. Women received their dead raised to life again. (Hebrews 11:33-35)

However, the next verses present a different reality:

> Others were tortured, not accepting deliverance, that they might obtain a better resurrection. Still others had trial of mockings and scourgings, yes, and of chains and imprisonment. They were stoned, they were sawn in two, were tempted, were slain with the sword. They wandered about in sheepskins and goatskins, being destitute, afflicted, tormented— of whom the world was not worthy. They wandered in deserts and mountains, in dens and caves of the earth. (Hebrews 11:35-38)

This passage clearly indicates that suffering is part of the Christian experience. There are times when our calling in Christ requires suffering. It requires sacrifice of comfort. It necessitates the facing of some burden. Again, this is not a matter of preference. It's a matter of the path God has plotted for our lives. Sacrifice and suffering may be part of the lines God draws for our lives in service to him.

Jesus forewarns us of this when he speaks in the Sermon on the Mount in Matthew 5:11-12: "Blessed are you when they revile and persecute you, and say all kinds of evil against you falsely for My sake. Rejoice and be exceedingly glad, for great is your reward in heaven, for so they persecuted the prophets who were before you." Jesus speaks about it in what he says to his disciples in

Matthew 16:24-25: "If anyone desires to come after Me, let him deny himself, and take up his cross, and follow Me. For whoever desires to save his life will lose it, but whoever loses his life for My sake will find it." In addition, God tells Ananias concerning Saul of Tarsus in Acts 9:15-16, "He is a chosen vessel of Mine to bear My name before Gentiles, kings, and the children of Israel. For I will show him how many things he must suffer for My name's sake." Paul reminds us of this in Acts 20:22-23 when he says to the Ephesian elders, "And see, now I go bound in the spirit to Jerusalem, not knowing the things that will happen to me there, except that the Holy Spirit testifies in every city, saying that chains and tribulations await me."

ACCEPT GOD'S UNPOPULAR PURPOSES

The life of clarity in Christ requires another acknowledgment. Namely: *I must accept and assert God's plan and purpose for my life in spite of the thoughts of others.*

When Peter declares Jesus to be the Christ and when Jesus commends Peter, everyone including Peter is fine. Everyone is fine with Jesus being the promised Messiah. Everyone is fine with Peter being the recipient of revelation, of Jesus building the church upon the revelation of his being the Christ, and of the keys of the kingdom being vested into their hands. It is only when Jesus starts clarifying the meaning of his Messiahship that Peter has a problem. Peter says "amen" to everything Jesus states until he starts talking about suffering and being killed. At this point Peter says, "Far be it from You, Lord; this shall not happen to You!" Peter can handle everything Jesus says up until he says he must suffer and be killed. Peter cannot handle those words. He cannot handle them not so much because of what they mean for Jesus, but because of what they mean for him.

Jesus' statement about suffering and being killed hits Peter on several levels. First, it hits him on the level of loss. Jesus' death will be a personal loss to Peter. Jesus will no longer be present for Peter. While we might think that level is enough, it goes even deeper for Peter—it hits him on the level of risk. If Jesus suffers and is killed, then Peter himself might suffer and be killed. We come to see this in what Jesus says to Peter in Matthew 16:24-26: "If anyone desires to come after Me, let him deny himself, and take up his cross, and follow Me. For whoever desires to save his life will lose it, but whoever loses his life for My sake will find it. For what profit is it to a man if he gains the whole world, and loses his own soul?" Within Jesus' statement about himself is a statement about the life ahead for Peter. His life will be one of suffering for the sake of righteousness. His life will be one of persecution. Peter cannot handle this. And because Peter cannot handle the implications for his life, he refutes its reality in Jesus' life.

The plan and purpose God has for our lives produce consequences and implications for those around us. Not everyone can handle the consequences and implications of God's work in our life for them. God's transformation provokes a change in everything connected to us. It gives rise to a renegotiation of terms of engagement and expectation, but some people can't deal with the renegotiated terms.

For example, when Joseph announces the divinely revealed intention for his life to his brothers, they cannot handle its implication for them (Genesis 50:15-21). When the girl with the spirit of divination is delivered, the men who profit from her oppression can't handle the implication of their "cash cow" being gone (Acts 16:16-23). If you come home talking about being saved, some people won't be able to handle the implications. They'll no longer have you as a pushover. You'll no longer want to do the things you used to do with them. They'll have one less reason to feel good about the path they travel, one that leads to death. They may need to find a new place to live. You'll refuse to go along with their questionable dealings on the job. They won't be able to count on you funding the dysfunctional behavior of the group any longer. Because they won't like the implications of your reality, they'll seek to deny its validity altogether. They'll try to make you think you're crazy. They'll try to get you to think there's something wrong with you. They'll try to diminish the worthiness of your claim by introducing doubt and inspiring ridicule.

When God directs the necessary path for us to travel and those around us can't handle it, we must be clear in our acceptance and assertion of God's will for our life. We can't allow their issues to become our issues. We can't allow their doubts to become our doubts. We can't allow their lack of belief to become our lack of belief. We can't allow their questioning to become our questioning. We can't allow their hesitancy to become our hesitancy. We can't allow their ambivalence to become our ambivalence. The clarity we have in God moves us to accept and to assert the plan, purpose, and path of God for our life.

God needs men and women whose clarity about who he has called them to be empowers them to withstand the thoughts and feelings of others. God needs men and women whose clarity refuses to allow the limitations of others' concepts to stifle who God is making us to be and what God is calling us to do.

ACCEPT THE REALITY OF OPPOSITION

Clarity in God's purpose for life emboldens the believer to make another claim: *I must accept and assert God's plan for my life in the face of satanic opposition.*

As Jesus spoke about his Messiahship requiring that he suffer and be killed, he is met with Peter's attempt to dismiss his statement. Even though it is Peter speaking, Jesus recognizes another voice. Hence he says, "Get behind me, Satan! You are an offense to me, for you are not mindful of the things of God, but the things of men." While it's Peter who makes the statement of contradiction, it's Satan who is named. Jesus is looking at Peter. It's Satan whom Jesus exposes. At the point of Peter's contradiction of Jesus' statement, Peter is under the influence of Satan. Jesus speaks to the spirit influencing Peter. He exposes the spirit behind Peter's words and actions. In so doing he alerts Peter to that in which he has participated. He has been a participant in satanic interference in what was designed to be a God thing. This was designed to be a God moment. It was to be a moment when God would be praised, celebrated, acknowledged, and surrendered to.

Our clarity about the things of God for our life is a major threat to the devil. He does everything he can to cause us to feel doubtful and uncertain. His mode of operation is to cast aspersion, sew suspicion, and create hesitancy. Hear him in the Garden of Eden: "Has God indeed said, 'You shall not eat of every tree of the garden'?" (Genesis 3:1). Hear him tell the woman, "You will not surely die. For God knows that in the day you eat of it your eyes will be opened, and you will be like God, knowing good and evil" (Genesis 3:4-5). Look at him with Jesus in the wilderness, where he says, "If you are the Son of God, command that these stones become bread" (Matthew 4:3), and "If You are the Son of God, throw yourself down. For it is written: 'He shall give his angels charge over you,' and, 'In their hands they shall bear you up, lest you dash your foot against a stone'" (Matthew 4:6).

His mode of operation has not changed. It is still the same. That is why we must be clear about who we are in God and in Christ. We must be clear about what God has spoken, revealed, birthed, called, and claimed for our life. When we are clear about the voice of God over our life and we accept and assert what God has spoken, we are able to recognize Satan speaking through human personality. It's a human mouth, but it's the devil's voice. Our clarity empowers and emboldens us to call the devil out by name. In calling the devil out, we expose him. We make individuals aware of their part in providing the devil access to what wasn't designed by God. Satan can't force his way in. He has to be allowed and admitted. He can't kick any doors down. The door has to be opened to him. It takes a person to open the door. The wise person is able to see this for what it is and call it out.

Maturity in Christ calls for clarity about the plan, purpose, and path of God for our life. As we walk in that clarity, Satan will use others around us to get us off track. He's able to use them because of their mindset. In Matthew 16:23 Jesus says, "You are not mindful of the things of God, but the things of men." Peter isn't listening to and processing Jesus' words with a spiritual ear. He is listening and processing with a natural ear. He isn't viewing things from God's perspective. He is viewing them from human perspective.

Whenever someone hears a spiritual truth from a natural perspective, there will always be a tendency to annul and deny what's been announced. The natural mind will never accept spiritual things. The natural eye will never correctly view spiritual things. Paul explains this in 1 Corinthians 2:10-14:

> The Spirit searches all things, yes, the deep things of God. For what man knows the things of a man except the spirit of the man which is in him? Even so no one knows the things of God except the Spirit of God. Now we have received, not the spirit of the world, but the Spirit who is from God, that we might know the things that have been freely given to us by God.
>
> These things we also speak, not in words which man's wisdom teaches but which the Holy Spirit teaches, comparing spiritual things with spiritual. But the natural man does not receive the things of the Spirit of God, for they are foolishness to him; nor can he know them, because they are spiritually discerned.

Peter felt that Jesus' words were foolishness. Why else would he dare tell Jesus "never"? In the natural mind, Jesus' words did not register. They did not compute. The things of God never compute in the natural mind. Bringing tithes and giving offerings as keys to open the windows of heaven doesn't make sense to the natural mind. The notion of gaining by losing, receiving by giving, and being great by being a servant is foolishness to the natural mind. The proposition of stepping out and going without knowing the name and location of the place you are headed is nonsense to the natural man and the natural mindset. Jesus Christ crucified is foolishness to Greeks and a stumbling block to Jews. God's thoughts are not our thoughts and his ways are not our ways. As high as the heavens are above the earth, so much higher are his thoughts than our thoughts and his ways than our ways.

When we begin to talk about the God reality of our life, not everyone is listening with a spiritual mindset. This includes Christians and saved people. Not all saved people listen with a spiritual mind. Not all saved people choose to operate with the mind of Christ. Some continue to live from a worldly perspective, and some choose to view spiritual matters from a natural point of view. Some have yet to accept the challenge of Paul in Romans 12:2: "Do not be conformed to this world, but be transformed by the renewing of your mind, that you may prove what is that good and acceptable and perfect will of God."

Jesus was clear enough about God and God's will for his life to know the devil's voice when he heard it. My friend, you must get to know God's voice for yourself. When you are clear about God's voice and when you are clear about God's will for your life, you are able to pick up the message from hell regardless of the face that's speaking it. You are able to look at the spirit behind the voice and the message and tell it, "Get behind me. I know God's plan for my life. I know God's purpose for my life. I know God's path for my life."

ACCEPT GOD'S WHOLE PLAN AND PURPOSE

Besides acknowledging that we must accept and assert the reality of sacrifice and suffering as part of the walk with Christ, that we must accept and assert the plan and purpose of God in spite of the contradictory thoughts of those close to us and in the face of satanic opposition, we must also acknowledge: *I must accept and assert the whole plan and purpose of God for my life.*

Jesus, having accepted and asserted the meaning behind his being the Messiah, is met by Peter, who seeks to contradict and deny the truth of Jesus' assertion. Peter does so in part because of selective hearing. Under the influence of the devil and from the construct of the natural mind, he can think only about one aspect of the reality Jesus announced. The devil amplifies a part of Jesus' revelation and mutes another part. Jesus doesn't stop with suffering and denying—he stops with resurrection. However, the devil amplifies the suffering and dying part. He abridges the resurrection but magnifies the sacrifice. He condenses the success. He maximizes the loss but minimizes the gain. He boosts the notion of defeat and reduces the notion of victory.

That's what the devil does when we approach the things of God with a natural mind. He amplifies only a part. He amplifies the bringing of the tithe and the giving of the offering and mutes the opening of the windows of heaven, the receiving of a poured-out blessing that we won't have room to receive, the rebuking of the devourer for our sake and the making of us a delightsome land. He expands our focus on those who do evil to us. He constricts the focus on God using our doing good to them to pour coals of fire on their head. The enemy intensifies our concentration on our not being able to live together or sleep together prior to marriage. He lessens our appreciation of the marriage bed being pure and undefiled and of our ability to be a witness to others in all things. He seeks to have us focus on the bumps and trials of the journey rather than the aim, end, and destination of the journey.

While Peter's focus is on suffering and being killed, which was short-term, Jesus is focused on the resurrection, which is long-term. Jesus juxtaposes the two approaches in Matthew 16:26-28: "What profit is it to a man if he gains the whole world, and loses his own soul? Or what will a man give in exchange for his soul? For the Son of Man will come in the glory of His Father with His angels, and then He will reward each according to his works. Assuredly, I say to you, there are some standing here who shall not taste death till they see the Son of Man coming in His kingdom."

Jesus is clear that this is a soul matter. This is a kingdom move. This is of cosmic consequence. It goes beyond preference and comfort. It's about the redemption of creation and the salvation of humanity. While there will be short-term sacrifice, there will be an eternal payoff. While there may be suffering and death, there is resurrection.

We must be clear about the full plan, purpose, and path of God. We can't get discouraged about the intermediate steps. We've got to look at the final destination. We've got to look at and listen to the long term:

His anger is but for a moment,
His favor is for life.
Weeping may endure for a night,
But joy comes in the morning. (Psalm 30:5)

And again, "Our light affliction, which is but for a moment, is working for us a far more exceeding and eternal weight of glory" (2 Corinthians 4:17). And again, "I consider that the sufferings of this present time are not worthy to be compared with the glory which shall be revealed in us" (Romans 8:18).

Jesus was clear about the whole plan, purpose, and path of God. While it included suffering and death, it did not end there. Even with the devil trying to end it in death, God had more in the plan and more for the path of Jesus. God had resurrection in the plan. God had victory over death, hell, and the grave in the plan. God had Jesus' exaltation in the plan. God had Jesus' return to the right hand of God the Father in the plan.

When Peter finally saw Jesus' clarity about the plan, purpose, and path of God, it caused him to be clearer about his own life and purpose. He in turn encourages us to be clear. Hear Peter say, "In his kindness God called you to share in his eternal glory by means of Christ Jesus. So after you have suffered a little while, he will restore, support, and strengthen you, and he will place you on a firm foundation" (1 Peter 5:10 NLT). We can be clear that God has called us to his eternal glory by means of Jesus Christ. I've been called to God's eternal glory. I've been called to God's unfading glory. I've been called to the glory of God. I know how it all ends. I can suffer a little while. After I've suffered a little while, God will restore, support, and strengthen. God will place me on a firm foundation. I'm clear about what's short-term and what's long-term. My tears are short-term. My burdens are short-term. My worries are short-term. My battles are short-term. My struggles are short-term. My frustrations and difficulties are short-term, but God's victory is long-term. God's strength is long-term. God's peace, joy, and glory are long-term. God's favor is long-term. God's grace is long-term. God's love is long-term.

Finally, God is calling men and women to live lives of clarity. God is calling men and women to accept and assert his claim on their lives and his will and vision for their lives.

5

I MUST BE DILIGENT

THE NECESSITY OF DILIGENCE

> Now as Jesus passed by, He saw a man who was blind from birth. And His disciples asked Him, saying, "Rabbi, who sinned, this man or his parents, that he was born blind?"
>
> Jesus answered, "Neither this man nor his parents sinned, but that the works of God should be revealed in him. I must work the works of Him who sent Me while it is day; the night is coming when no one can work. As long as I am in the world, I am the light of the world." (John 9:1-5)

The life of Jesus reveals that God's call and God's claim on the believer's life are imperative in nature and not simply indicative. Hence, maturity in Christ includes recognizing that the Christian life is, by necessity, a life of focus, of dynamic progression, of direction, and of clarity. Yet more is required. There is another necessary characteristic of the mature Christian. It is that of diligence. Diligence involves careful and persistent work or effort. It also involves a zealous and careful nature in one's actions and work. Diligence is a combination of zeal and care. The God-directed life must be pursued with diligence.

A LIFE OF DISCERNMENT

Jesus and the disciples are in Jerusalem. They come across a man who was blind from birth. The disciples, operating under the conventional wisdom that the man's condition was the result of either the sins of his parents or his own sins while in the womb, ask Jesus the question about who sinned. Jesus responds that neither sinned. It happened so that the power of God could be seen in him. He continues, saying, "I must work the works of Him who sent Me while it is day; the night is coming when no one can work. As long as I am in the world, I am the light of the world."

In saying this, Jesus demonstrates that the necessary life is one that says: *I must live a life of discernment.*

Jesus' statement "I must work the work of Him who sent Me while it is day" comes in the context of responding to his disciples' question about the cause of the man's blindness. They are questioning Jesus out of a sense of occasion. The disciples view the occasion of seeing the blind man as an occasion for assigning blame. They see it as an occasion for theological discourse around the reason for the man's suffering. They view the moment as an opportunity for reflection on the nature of bad things happening to good people.

Jesus answers by saying, "Neither this man nor his parents sinned, but that the works of God should be revealed in him." In the presence of the man and his condition of blindness, Jesus and the disciples are confronted with a circumstance that requires discernment. While the disciples believe the man's condition to be a moment for reflection on the nature of suffering, Jesus understands it to be a moment for revelation of God's power within the man. Jesus looks at the same moment differently. While all the disciples can see is a moment of speculation and assigning blame, Jesus sees the moment as a moment of service through which the power of God will be revealed in the man's healing and liberation.

Under the direction of God, Jesus and the disciples' path intersects with the blind man's path. At issue is the understanding of such an intersection. While the disciples are thinking about why the man is in his condition, Jesus is thinking about why God has directed their paths to intersect. With the disciples thinking about the why of the man's condition, Jesus is thinking about the why of their intersection and present interaction.

In Jesus' statement, the cause of the man's blindness is secondary to the purpose of God in their coming across the blind man. God has a work in mind within the blind man's circumstance that will reveal God's power. Jesus is present so the power of God may be seen.

Jesus demonstrates the necessity of discerning the God-meaning of the moment. Since God has directed their paths to cross, Jesus seeks to know and carry out the God-purpose for the moment presented. He doesn't want to be in a God-directed moment and miss its meaning. He doesn't want to be involved in a pursuit that is contrary to the purpose for which he is present.

The necessary Christian life is a life of diligence informed by discernment. It is a life whose carefulness is influenced by discerning the will of God in the moment. It is a life that seeks to be led by God-meaning. It is a life that asks these questions: What does God desire to reveal in this encounter? What does God want to show through this interaction? What does God seek to demonstrate in this circumstance?

As we seek to live God-directed lives, we must know that God has a reason for every way in which he directs us. God gives no random direction. Every direction has a purpose. Every encounter has a meaning. It is necessary that we discern the meaning. It is imperative that we understand the purpose. Getting to a place and then not knowing what we are to do in that place does the kingdom no good. We must be able to know why we are where we are. Fulfilling the assignment of God for our life is not just getting to the assigned place. It is operating within the purpose God has for the place where he's assigned us.

Jesus correctly understood why the blind man's path intersected with his. It was so the power of God might be seen. Wherever the Lord directs us, there is an aspect of revelation tied to it. The better question of discernment is what aspect of God's power God wants to reveal.

The discernment of the meaning of the moment causes Jesus to know that this is not accidental. This is purposeful. He is there for a reason and that reason is tied to his assignment. It is a part of the work to which he's been called.

A SENSE OF URGENCY

Jesus continues, saying, "I must work the works of Him who sent Me while it is day; the night is coming when no man can work." This is not only saying I must live a discerning life. It is also saying: *I must live with a sense of urgency.*

Jesus speaks of the necessity of working his assignment while it is day. Night is coming when no one can work. Jesus is stressing the urgency of his work. He must get about doing his work because there is a time frame in which it must be done. There is a limit on the time available to him. Time is of the essence. He must do what he can quickly because he has been given a window of time. A time will come when he won't be able to do it. The window will be closed. The door will be shut. The opportunity will disappear.

The mature Christian is one who understands the urgency of the time he or she has been given in which to live. As believers in the Lord, we must know that we don't have forever to do what the Lord is calling us to do. Our time on this earth is not limitless but limited. We don't have time to waste. With each day that passes, we have one less day upon the earth. With each day that comes, we have one less day in our future. Effective living within the things of God is not just realizing the purpose of God but also realizing the urgency of fulfilling the purpose of God.

We must work while it is day, while we have the time, and while we have the opportunity. We must give while we have the resources, lead while we have the influence, learn while we have the power of recall and remembrance, and spend time with our children while they're young. They won't be young forever. We must love and enjoy our spouse. He or she won't be around forever. We must honor our parents while we have the time because they won't live forever.

Diligence entails approaching life and the claims of God on our life with a sense of urgency. It causes us to recognize that we must do this while we have the chance. We must pursue while we have the opportunity. We must seize the moment while it's within our reach. We don't have time to waste. The day is fleeting. The time is moving quickly. The moment is short-lived.

Urgency moves us to say to ourselves, "I must do this within the time God is giving me. The only time I know God is giving me is right now." We may hope God will give us more time, but the only time we know God is giving us is this moment. Our life must be lived from a standpoint that asserts, "I can't waste what I have right now. I can't blow the time I have right now. I can't be careless with the opportunity I have right now. I can't misuse the moment I have right now. I can't squander the shot God has presented me right now. I can't fritter away the favor God has given me right now."

We must work the work now. We must answer the call now. We must fulfill the assignment and pursue the path now. We must fight the fight now. We must make the move and take the journey now. We must make the change now. We must close the door now.

The mature Christian knows he or she does not have time to waste. Time is not on our side. Each second that ticks by is a second we've lost if we're not doing what we're supposed to be doing. We don't have time to rest on our laurels. We don't have time to grow complacent. We don't have time to sit in yesterday or last year. That was then and this is now. Now, we must work, serve, grow, change, learn, adapt, and improve. Now, we must sacrifice. We won't have this now for very long. Night is coming.

If you are still reading this, God is impressing on you the necessity of urgency. He's telling you that you don't have time to waste. In fact, you have less time than you've ever had before. Perhaps you've grown complacent and stale. He's trying to shake you out of your lethargy. He's trying to move you into diligence. He's showing you that the time of your life is calling. He's revealing to you the meaning of the moment. He's imploring you to pursue it with urgency. He's challenging you to make haste in its direction. Night is coming.

Maximize Every Moment

Jesus speaks of discernment and urgency. Then he says, "As long as I am in the world, I am the light of the world." The NLT translates John 9:5 this way: "But while I am here in the world, I am the light of the world." The necessary life is one that asserts not only the necessity of living a life of discernment and of urgency but also one that asserts: *I must live a life of maximization.*

Jesus says, "While I am here." He doesn't get tied down by night coming. He focuses on the day existing. He focuses on the chance he has. He can't change when he won't be here. All he can do is maximize the time while he is here. While he is here, he is the light of the world. While he is here, he has the power he has. While he is here, he will be who he is supposed to be. While he is here, he will do what he is supposed to do. While he is here, he will work what he is supposed to work. He will maximize the moment he has.

The life of diligence is the life of maximizing the moment we have. It is the life that seeks to make the most of all the time we have. We may not know how much time we have, but we can make the most of what we have. The maximized life says, "While I am here, I'm going to do what I'm supposed to do. While I am here, I'm going to pursue what I'm supposed to pursue. While I am here, I'm going to be everything God wants me to be. While I am here, I'm going to go everywhere God wants me to go. While I am here, I'm going to possess everything God wants me to possess. While I am here, I'm going to learn what I'm supposed to learn. While I am here, I'm going to make the most of the time I have."

Jesus maximizes the moment. In the encounter in John 9, he places mud on the blind man's eyes and tells him to go wash in the pool of Siloam. The man could have wasted a lot of time, but he senses the moment with which he's been presented. So he goes and washes. As a result, he comes back seeing. Now the blind man is the sighted man. As the neighbors view the sighted man, they miss the moment. Rather than seeing the power of God, his parents, out of fear of the Jews who could put them out of the synagogue, miss the moment of celebrating their son's healing by Jesus.

The blind but now sighted man does not miss his moment. He maximizes the moment by declaring the power of God: "One thing I know: that though I was blind, now I see. . . . He has opened my eyes! Now we know that God does not hear sinners; but if anyone is a worshiper of God and does His will, He hears him. Since the world began it has been unheard of that anyone opened the eyes of one who was born blind. If this Man were not from God, He could do nothing" (John 9:25, 30-33). The man maximizes his moment of worshiping Jesus as the Son of God, declaring, "Lord, I believe."

Jesus and the once blind but now sighted man challenge us to maximize the moment. Don't miss the moment. Maximize the moment as did Jesus. When Satan sought to cancel his moments, even then Jesus was maximizing. At Calvary Satan tried to cancel Jesus' moment, but Jesus made the most of the moment. He used it to issue a word of forgiveness and offer a thief paradise. He used the moment to secure the caretaking of his mother by John. He used the moment to quench his thirst for the Scriptures' fulfillment. He used the moment to provide the currency for our redemption, taking every one of our sins and nailing them to the tree. He used the moment to take the full wrath of God upon himself and face every charge and ordinance that was against us. He used the moment to take our place, punishment, and penalty. And even there, at Calvary, somebody saw the power of God. A Roman centurion saw the power and declared, "Truly this was the Son of God!" (Matthew 27:54).

Jesus also maximized the moments of his death. From his death on Friday to his burial, even then Jesus maximized his moment by descending into hell, preaching to the spirits held captive, and taking the keys of death and hell. Early Sunday morning, God the Father showed his power by raising Jesus from the dead. He displayed his power by exalting Jesus to the right hand of the throne of God.

Jesus maximized his moments and lived a diligent life and this empowered him to save, deliver, and transform us.

I challenge you to make up in your mind that while you're here, you'll do what you're supposed to do. I challenge you to live a diligent life. I challenge you to discern the time. I challenge you to redeem the time. I challenge you to maximize the time.

6

I MUST YIELD TO GOD'S WILL

THE NECESSITY OF YIELDING

"Up, let's be going. Look, my betrayer is here!"

And even as Jesus said this, Judas, one of the twelve disciples, arrived with a crowd of men armed with swords and clubs. They had been sent by the leading priests and elders of the people. The traitor, Judas, had given them a prearranged signal: "You will know which one to arrest when I greet him with a kiss." So Judas came straight to Jesus. "Greetings, Rabbi!" he exclaimed and gave him the kiss.

Jesus said, "My friend, go ahead and do what you have come for."

Then the others grabbed Jesus and arrested him. But one of the men with Jesus pulled out his sword and struck the high priest's slave, slashing off his ear.

"Put away your sword," Jesus told him. "Those who use the sword will die by the sword. Don't you realize that I could ask my Father for thousands of angels to protect us, and he would send them instantly? But if I did, how would the Scriptures be fulfilled that describe what must happen now?" (Matthew 26:46-54 NLT)

T hroughout the past five chapters, we have been examining the "I must" and "he must" statements made by and about Jesus. From them we have learned that the necessary life to which we are called is a God-focused, dynamically progressive, and God-directed life lived in clarity and in diligence.

It must be said that this life is lived in constant tension. A focused, progressive, and God-directed life lived in clarity and diligence is a tension-filled life. It is a life that experiences competing forces pulling on it as it seeks to fulfill God's purpose. The primary tension is that of fighting against the will of God and of yielding to the will of God. It is that of rebellion and obedience. When it comes to living a life that is God-focused, dynamically progressive, and God-directed in clarity and urgency, there is the "must" of yielding.

The text before us reveals the tension of a life that seeks to live in God's purpose. Jesus has instituted what we call the Lord's Supper in the upper room. He has foretold Peter's threefold denial. He has spent time with God to come to terms with God's will for his life. As Jesus speaks to the disciples, Judas, along with an armed mob of men, approaches Jesus. Judas betrays Jesus using a sign of affection—a kiss. Jesus tells Judas to do what he came to do. As the men grab Jesus, Peter pulls out his sword and cuts off the ear of the high priest's slave. Jesus looks at Peter and tells him to put away his sword, that those who live by the sword die by the sword, that if he wanted he could ask his Father for thousands of angels to protect them, but if he did the Scriptures wouldn't be fulfilled. He concludes by telling Peter it must happen this way.

As the rising action of the drama of redemption speeds to a climax, we are given two responses to the lived-out will of God. On the one hand there is Peter, who pulls out his sword and cuts the ear off a soldier. On the other hand there is Jesus, who receives Judas's deceitful kiss and tells him to do what he came to do. In Peter there is resistance to what's happening. In Jesus there is a yielding to what's happening. With the slicing off of the slave's ear, Peter is saying, "It doesn't have to be this way." Jesus says, "It must happen this way."

REFUSE TO AVOID GOD'S PURPOSES

When it comes to living within the will of God, when it comes to living a God-directed life in clarity and urgency, yielding is a necessity. I must yield to the will of God. By saying, "It must happen this way," Jesus asserts that the yielded life is the life that says: *I must refuse to use my resources to avoid God's purpose for my life.*

Jesus speaks to two entities. The first is Peter. He tells Peter, "Don't you realize that I could ask my Father for thousands of angels to protect us, and he would send them instantly? But if I did, how would the Scriptures be fulfilled that describe what must happen now?" As Jesus is arrested, he has a choice before him. Does he use what is at his disposal to avoid being arrested? Does he exercise his authority, his power, his influence to sidestep or frustrate the process of God for his life? If he wanted to, he could call for angelic assistance and it would be given. But if he did that, he would run counter to the purpose for which he had been sent into the world.

On the one hand, he can use what is available to him to avoid the pain of God's purposeful process for his life. On the other, he can refuse to use what is available to him and yield to God's purposeful process. Jesus chooses to yield to God's purposeful process. Out of that choice he then refuses to use what is available to him to avoid the pain of the process.

Yielding to the will of God for our lives often involves refusing to use what we could use, because using our resources opposes God's way for us. Yielding to the will of God may call for us to refuse to use some things that make us feel good and that we feel justified in using. Calling down angels may have made Jesus feel good. In his humanity, Jesus may have even felt justified in calling them down. However, this would have run contrary to the path God had established for Jesus.

Yielding to the will and way of God may sometimes require that we refuse to use what makes us feel good and justified to stay on the path God has established for our life. It may mean refusing to strike back at the one who hurt us. It may mean refusing to say certain things even when saying them would make us look better. It may mean staying put and not moving when moving would make us feel better.

In each case, the issue is what we live for. What is the basis of our life? Is the basis for our life how we look and feel, or is it pursuing the will of God and being in the will of God? When being in the will of God is the basis for how we live our life, sometimes we have to discount how we look and how we feel. Sometimes being in the will of God requires that we look foolish to the world. Sometimes being in the will of God means we look weak and feel vulnerable to the world. In those times, we have to refuse to use what we could use to make us look and feel differently. We have to deny ourselves the weaponry we could employ. We do so because our desire for the will of God is greater than how we look to people and how we feel.

EXERCISE PATIENCE IN GOD'S PROCESS

There is another assertion that the yielded life makes. It is: *I must exercise patience in God's process.*

After speaking to Peter, Jesus speaks to the crowd. He asks why they've come at him the way they have. He asks why they didn't come at him while he was teaching in the temple every day. He informs them that the only reason they are coming at him now is because God is fulfilling his word. As I indicated in chapter one, since the age of twelve

Jesus has been about the Father's business. Since at least the age of twelve Jesus has had an idea of what the Father desired of him.

Imagine that you're Jesus. From as early as age twelve you've lived under the awareness that you've come to give your life as a sacrifice for the world. For twenty-one years you've lived your life for an hour to come to pass. For twenty-one years you've anticipated the moments of redemption. For twenty-one years you've carried the weight of knowing your life is headed to a violent though victorious conclusion. Every time you taught in the temple, you could have been taken. Each time it didn't happen, you were taken closer to your place and purpose.

Jesus has waited for this hour. The hour has finally come. Here Jesus faces Judas and the mob. Judas deceitfully kisses Jesus. The mob grabs Jesus and roughs him up. Rather than fight back, Jesus simply yields. He faces them with patience. In Greek, one of the words for "patience" is *hypomonē*. It means "to stand under." Jesus is willing to stand under what is before him. His standing under the voice of God and living within the will of God cause him to stand under the circumstance that confronts him. His yielding to it is his willingness to stand under it. He stands under the circumstance because he is under the voice of God. He is under the word of God for his life. His being under the word of God for his life enables him to stand under the situation before him.

Yielding to the will of God for our lives requires patience. It necessitates our willingness to stand under situations demanded by being in the will of God. In Jesus' case, it meant standing under the experience of betrayal. It meant standing under the experience of an angry mob. It meant standing under the experience of false accusation. It meant standing under the experience of mistrial and wrongful conviction. It included the exercise of patience.

Our yielding to the will of God may mean standing under the experience of betrayal, of rejection, of isolation, of illness, or of being misunderstood. Actively living within the will of God may require that our patience be exercised. Exercising patience within the will of God is the ability to say that, if this must be, then I'll take it knowing I can take it. I can face it. I can bear it. I can carry it. I can stand under it. I may not like it or even understand it, but I will stand under it because I must.

With Peter aggressively fighting against Judas and the mob, Jesus patiently yields to them. He does so because he realizes that this is God's way. This is the way he must take. This is the path set before him. This is a part of the business he has been about since the age of twelve.

TAKE GOD'S WAY AS YOUR WAY

The life that realizes the necessity of yielding is not simply the life that says, "I must refuse to use my resources to avoid God's purpose for my life," and, "I must exercise patience in God's process." It is also the life that says: *I must take God's way to be my way.*

In Matthew 26:56, Jesus reminds the mob that their seizure of him at this particular point in time is happening because God is fulfilling the word proclaimed by the prophets. Their access to Jesus is permitted because this is God's way for Jesus at this point in time. They were denied access to Jesus earlier because it wasn't God's time for that part of the plan. They have access to him now because this is the time for this part of the redemption plan to be put into effect.

Jesus knows what Peter and the crowd do not know. This is all a part of God's plan. He has forewarned the disciples of this on several occasions. He has told them he would be betrayed into the hands of sinful men. In Matthew 26:21 and 23, in the upper room, he has gone even further and alerted them that the betrayer is among them. This is all part of God's plan. It is God's way of moving along the course of redemption and salvation.

With that in mind, Jesus consciously chooses to yield to God's way. He willingly gives himself to God's way. Having given himself to God's way, he gives himself to Judas and the mob. Remember that Jesus has said, "No one takes [my life] from Me, but I lay it down of Myself. I have power to lay it down, and I have power to take it again" (John 10:18).

The life of yielding is the life that consciously decides to take God's way. It is to give ourselves to God. In giving ourselves to God, we give ourselves to the way God has established. Sometimes the way God establishes includes the enemy having access to us. Sometimes it includes the enemy having an opportunity to lay a hand on us. Sometimes it involves our appearing weak in comparison to that which is against us.

When Jesus yields to Judas and the mob, the disciples are placed in the position of making a choice. Will they stay with Jesus? Will they walk with Jesus in this part of his life? Will they hang with Jesus through this episode in the redemption story? Will Thomas, who volunteered in John 11:16 to go to Jerusalem with Jesus so he could die with him, actually live up to his word? The end of Matthew 26:56 answers the question. It reads, "Then all the disciples forsook Him and fled."

When we choose to surrender our life to the will of God and actively yield to his way for us, we also set up the situation for those around us to make a choice. Those around us must choose whether or not they can stand with us. They must choose to continue or to discontinue the journey with us. Their choice will be based on who they are and what they believe they can stand. Not everybody can handle the implications of our life of surrender to God. Not everybody can handle the pressure that comes on the path God may call us to travel. To be sure, they can handle the benefits of our life with God. The disciples could handle the perks that came with being with Jesus. They could handle the miraculous feedings. They could handle his calming the sea and walking on water. They could handle his coming to their rescue. They could handle standing with him as he displayed his power among the people. They could handle those times with him. But this is a different scenario. Jesus is giving himself up willingly to Judas and the mob. They haven't signed up for this part. They can't handle how they might be seen or treated by being identified with Jesus at this stage of his walk.

Likewise, people around us can handle being with us when the benefits are obvious. They can hang with us when things are coming to them and happening for them as a result of being in our orbit. But when our following God and doing what we must do threaten their benefit or their comfort, they may not be able to handle that. At that point they will make a choice. Like the disciples, they will desert us and flee.

This is no surprise to Jesus. He knew it would be so. He foretold it to them in the upper room. In Matthew 26:31 Jesus said, "Tonight all of you will desert me. For the Scriptures say, 'God will strike the Shepherd, and the sheep of the flock will be scattered'" (NLT).

FACE SOME THINGS ALONE

In John 16:32 Jesus says, "The time is coming—indeed it's here now—when you will be scattered, each one going his own way, leaving me alone" (NLT). Here Jesus unveils still another assertion concerning the yielded life: *I must face some things alone.*

Jesus knew the disciples. He knew they wouldn't be able to travel this part of the journey with him. They would leave him and flee. He yielded to their desertion. He didn't try to get them to stay. He didn't ask where they were going. He didn't holler at them to come back. He knew he would have to face this part without them.

When we decide to give ourselves fully to the Lord's work, will, and way, not everybody will choose to travel in that direction. Not everybody can and will choose the full way of the Lord. Some, when faced with the decision to go the Lord's way or their own way, will choose to go their own way. They'll choose the less complicated way. They'll choose the less sacrificial way. They'll choose the less painful way. They'll choose the less confining way. They'll choose the less difficult way.

Like Jesus, you may find yourself by yourself, but there is something Jesus knew. In those times when walking in the will of God forces a separation from others, you may be by yourself, but you're not alone. Again in John 16:32, Jesus says, "Yet I am not alone because the Father is with me" (NLT). When the disciples deserted Jesus and fled,

Jesus was not alone in the situation. Unseen by the casual observer, unperceived by Judas, unimagined by the mob, and undetected by the chief priests and elders, God the Father was with Jesus. Jesus had placed himself in the will of God. He'd prayed himself into the will of God. Having prayed himself into the will of God, he put himself in the position for God the Father to stand with him. When we put ourselves in the will of God, we position ourselves for God to stand with us. When we pray, "Not my will but yours be done," we position ourselves for God to stand with us. At that point it doesn't matter who stays or who goes. All that matters is that God is standing with us.

God the Father stands with Jesus, giving him strength for this part of the Father's business. God the Father stands with Jesus as Jesus stands before the Sanhedrin. God the Father stands with Jesus as Jesus stands before Pontius Pilate. God the Father stands with Jesus as Jesus is beaten and scourged with a lead-tipped whip. God the Father is with Jesus as they nail him to the cross. God the Father is with Jesus as he dies for our sin.

Even when the ugliness of sin is upon Jesus and the Father, who can't look at sin, turns his head and Jesus feels forsaken, in reality God the Father is still there. He's still there to give Jesus the power to die a redemptive death. He's still there to empower Jesus to cancel the ordinances and laws that were against us, to inspire Jesus to see the business all the way through. He's still there to the very end so Jesus can cry out, "It is finished," and "Father, into Your hands I commit My spirit" (Luke 23:46). The Father is there when they take Jesus off the cross and bury him in Joseph's tomb. The Father is there when Jesus descends into hell and preaches to the spirits held captive. Early Sunday morning, the Father is there to raise Jesus from the dead.

When you yield to the will of God, God will stand by you and with you. God will be by your side. You'll never walk alone because he'll walk with you. He'll assure you that he's in control and is working all things together for your good.

EPILOGUE

Contrary to those who live optional, accidental, and haphazard lives, the believer in Christ is challenged to live with a sense of divine necessity. It is to live a "must" life in a "maybe" world. This is the life given to us by Christ. In both word and deed, he demonstrates the characteristics of living a "must" life. In the course of living in a "maybe" world, we should call to mind Christ's "must" statements and make them our own. In a "maybe" world, we should remember that we are called to be set apart by electing to submit to the teachings of Jesus.

Living a "must" life is a life of *focus*. It is a life that affirms:

- I must keep the necessity of my existence in focus.
- I must keep the intentionality of life in focus.
- I must keep my relationship with God in focus.
- I must keep the calling I am to pursue in focus.

Living a "must" life is a life of *progression*. It is a life that affirms:

- I must accept the dynamic nature of life in Christ.
- I must live by assignment and not by personal preference.
- I must live from the standpoint of continuity regardless of my context.

Living a "must" life is a life of *direction*. It is a life that affirms:

- I must follow God's direction to places others would avoid.
- I must engage those whom others would shun.
- I must follow God into that which is greater than what others can understand.

Living a "must" life is a life of *clarity*. It is a life that affirms:

- I must accept the reality of suffering and sacrifice as a part of my walk with Christ.
- I must assert God's plan and purpose in spite of the thoughts of others.
- I must assert God's plan in the face of satanic opposition.
- I must assert God's whole plan and purpose for my life.

Living a "must" life is a life of *diligence*. It is a life that affirms:

- I must live a life of discernment.
- I must live with a sense of urgency.
- I must maximize the moments I have.

Living a "must" life is a life that *yields* to God. It is a life that affirms:

- I must refuse attempts to avoid God's purpose for my life.
- I must exercise patience in God's process.
- I must take God's way to be my way.
- I must face some things alone.

This path is not without its challenges. However, Christ's example assures us that, by following it, we realize God's purpose for our lives and experience God's power and pleasure in wonderful ways.

QUESTIONS FOR REFLECTION AND DISCUSSION

The following questions engage with each chapter's examination of the "must" statements of and about Jesus in the Gospels. They may be used for either individual reflection or group discussion to become acquainted with the sense of "the necessary" that a life in Christ provokes and provides. This challenges the postmodern sense that a life in Christ is all about choice, personal preference, and entitlement. What that means is that we will come to understand that life in Christ and with Christ is less about what we could do and more about what we must do. Freedom in Christ does not make the desires and demands of Christ of us and for us optional. Rather, freedom in Christ disentangles us so we are able to respond to that which is necessary for us from Christ and in Christ.

CHAPTER 1: I MUST FOCUS

Of all the things Christ wants for us, loving Him and focusing our attention on Him are the most important.

CHARLES STANLEY

Through examination of Luke 2:40-52, the story of Jesus in the temple, we are introduced to the idea of focusing on the necessity of our existence, on the intentionality of our life, on the primacy of our relationship with God, and on the calling we are to pursue.

| 1. Is there a time in your life when you lost focus?

| 2. In retrospect, why did you lose focus?

| 3. What about now? What have you lost focus of?

4. What can you do or what resources can you use to keep focus?

5. What are you called to do?

6. How are purpose and focus connected?

7. What are some necessary steps you can take or strategies you can pursue to achieve and maintain focus?

CHAPTER 2: I MUST PROGRESS

We all want progress, but progress means getting nearer to and actually being in the place where God desires you to be and accomplishing the tasks God has set for you.

ANONYMOUS

Through examination of Luke 4:38-44, we come to see that the life in Christ is necessarily dynamically progressive in nature and requires that life be lived from the perspective of assignment, not preference, and continuity regardless of context.

| 1. Are you a static or dynamic Christian?

| 2. How do you know? Support your response with evidence.

| 3. How is Christian maturity to be measured?

4. Have you reflected on your assignment and your pursuit of it?

5. What assignments have you avoided and for what reasons?

6. How did avoidance of that assignment impede your growth?

7. How persistent are you in carrying out your assignment when you experience obstacles and conflicts?

CHAPTER 3: I MUST BE DIRECTED

Is it for you to lead Jesus to where you want to go,
or for Him to lead you where He wants you to be?

ANONYMOUS

Through examination of John 4:1-30, the story of Jesus and the woman of Samaria, we see the life of Jesus through the lens of being directed by God. As such, we come to know that a God-directed life will cause us to go to places others would avoid, to engage those others would shun, and to participate in that which is greater than what others can see.

1. Has it been easy or difficult for you to follow the direction of God?

2. What makes it easy or difficult?

3. How have you resisted the direction of God?

4. Has God's direction led you to places and people others have shunned?

5. How important is it to you that people understand where God is leading you?

6. Can you share the experience of a time when God worked wonders through the unconventional, unfamiliar, unusual, and uncommon?

7. Name three people you have helped through challenging situations.

CHAPTER 4: I MUST BE CLEAR

Clarity affords focus.

ANDREW COBURN

Through examination of Matthew 16:13-27, we see Jesus operating in and asserting clarity. With this we discover that clarity empowers us to accept and assert the reality of sacrifice and suffering as part of our walk with Christ, requires us to accept and assert God's plan and purpose in spite of the thoughts of others, and demands that we accept and assert the whole plan and purpose of God for our life.

1. Have you received clarity on God's plan and purpose for your life?

2. How do you view suffering?

3. Is suffering a sign of God's disfavor?

4. What does your denomination or theology teach you about suffering?

5. Can suffering build Christian character or cause a loss of faith?

6. How can you begin to live a life of clarity today?

7. Name three ways you seek God's clarity.

CHAPTER 5: I MUST BE DILIGENT

The Lord help me to press after God forever.

DAVID BRAINERD

Through examination of John 9:1-5, we observe Jesus' diligence in both word and deed. This causes us to realize that the call to a life of diligence is the call to discernment, to live with a sense of urgency, and to maximize the moments we have.

| 1. Do you have Christian discernment?

| 2. How do you exercise discernment?

| 3. Can discernment help you see the causality of intersections in your life?

4. Do you know why you are where you are?

5. Are you living with a sense of urgency?

6. How are you maximizing your moments?

7. How would you define Christian diligence?

CHAPTER 6: I MUST YIELD TO GOD'S WILL

*Too many Christians have a commitment of convenience.
They'll stay faithful as long as it's safe and doesn't
involve risk, rejection, or criticism. Instead of
standing alone in the face of challenge or temptation,
they check to see which way their friends are going.*

CHARLES STANLEY

Through examination of Matthew 26:46-56, the betrayal and arrest of Jesus, we are challenged by the characteristics of a life that yields to the will of God. We see that the yielded life is the life in which we refuse to use what we could use to avoid God's purpose for our life, exercise patience in God's process, take God's way, and are willing to face some things alone being secured by God's presence.

1. In what areas of your life are you struggling against yielding to the will of God?

2. Identify one area in which you have yielded to the will of God.

3. How relevant for you is the statement, "I must refuse to use what I could use to avoid God's purpose for my life"?

4. Was there an aha moment in this book, *Necessary Christianity*, for you? What was it?

5. Name a person with whom you feel comfortable confiding your deepest secrets.

6. What do you think is your greatest impediment to living a more committed life for Christ?

7. Do you have an accountability partner who can help you stay in the Word of God?

ABOUT THE AUTHOR

Bishop Claude Richard Alexander Jr. has pastored The Park Church in Charlotte, North Carolina, since 1990. He earned a bachelor's degree from Morehouse College, a master of divinity from Pittsburgh Theological Seminary, and a doctor of ministry from Gordon-Conwell Theological Seminary. He began pastoring his first church in 1987 and was ordained a bishop in 2008. Under his leadership, The Park Church has grown from one local congregation of six hundred members to a global ministry of thousands with three locations and weekly international reach. Bishop Alexander has gained increasing presence in the media, reaching a potential audience of more than two million viewers each week through his live-streamed sermons.

A leader among both Christian and civic organizations, he has consistently been listed among the most influential persons in Charlotte, North Carolina. Bishop

Alexander has worked with government and community officials to address the community's most critical issues. Over the years, he has served as a board member of the Urban League of Central Carolinas, United Way, the Arts and Science Council, the NAACP Educational Committee, the Harvey B. Gantt Center for African American Arts and Culture, and the Community Building Initiative. Currently, he serves on the boards of Charlotte Center City Partners, Christianity Today, Mission America Coalition, Council for Christian Colleges & Universities, InterVarsity Christian Fellowship, and Movement.Org. He is the chair of Gordon-Conwell Theological Seminary board of trustees and the second-presiding bishop of the Kingdom Association of Covenant Pastors. He is a past president of the Hampton University Ministers Conference, the oldest and largest interdenominational gathering of African American clergy in the United States.

Bishop Alexander and his wife, Dr. Kimberly Nash Alexander, have been married since 1993. They have two daughters, Camryn and Carsyn.

https://bishopclaudealexander.org
https://theparkministries.org